UNITED NATIONS CONFERENCE ON TRADE AND DEVELOPMENT

SCOPE AND DEFINITION

UNCTAD Series on Issues in International Investment
Agreements II

UNITED NATIONS
New York and Geneva, 2011

NOTE

As the focal point in the United Nations system for investment and technology, and building on 30 years of experience in these areas, UNCTAD, through the Division on Investment and Enterprise (DIAE), promotes understanding of key issues, particularly matters related to foreign direct investment (FDI). DIAE assists developing countries in attracting and benefiting from FDI by building their productive capacities, enhancing their international competitiveness and raising awareness about the relationship between investment and sustainable development. The emphasis is on an integrated policy approach to investment and enterprise development.

The term "country" as used in this study also refers, as appropriate, to territories or areas. The designations employed and the presentation of the material do not imply the expression of any opinion whatsoever on the part of the Secretariat of the United Nations concerning the legal status of any country, territory, city or area or of its authorities, or concerning the delimitation of its frontiers or boundaries. In addition, the designations of country groups are intended solely for statistical or analytical convenience and do not necessarily express a judgment about the stage of development reached by a particular country or area in the development process.

The following symbols have been used in the tables:

Two dots (..) indicate that data are not available or are not separately reported.

Rows in tables have been omitted in those cases where no data are available for any of the elements in the row.

A dash (-) indicates that the item is equal to zero or its value is negligible.

A blank in a table indicates that the item is not applicable.

A slash (/) between dates representing years, e.g. 1994/1995, indicates a financial year.

Use of a hyphen (-) between dates representing years, e.g. 1994-1995, signifies the full period involved, including the beginning and end years.

Reference to "dollars" ($) means United States dollars, unless otherwise indicated.

Annual rates of growth or change, unless otherwise stated, refer to annual compound rates.

Details and percentages in tables do not necessarily add to totals because of rounding.

The material contained in this study may be freely quoted with appropriate acknowledgement.

UNCTAD/DIAE/IA/2010/2

UNITED NATIONS PUBLICATION
Sales No. E.11.II.D.9
ISBN 978-92-1-112815-4

PREFACE

This volume is part of a series of revised editions – *sequels* – to UNCTAD's "Series on Issues in International Investment Agreements". The first generation of this series (also called the "Pink Series") was published between 1999 and 2005 as part of UNCTAD's work programme on international investment agreements (IIAs). It aimed at assisting developing countries to participate as effectively as possible in international investment rulemaking at the bilateral, regional, plurilateral and multilateral levels. The series sought to provide balanced analyses of issues that may arise in discussions about IIAs, and has since then become a standard reference tool for IIA negotiators, policymakers, the private sector, academia and other stakeholders.

Since the publication of the first generation of the Pink Series, the world of IIAs has changed tremendously. In terms of numbers, the IIAs' universe has grown, and continues to do so – albeit to a lesser degree. Also, the impact of IIAs has evolved. Many investor-State dispute settlement (ISDS) cases have brought to light unanticipated – and partially undesired – side effects of IIAs. With its expansive – and sometimes contradictory – interpretations, the arbitral interpretation process has created a new learning environment for countries and, in particular, for IIA negotiators. Issues of transparency, predictability and policy space have come to the forefront of the debate. So has the objective of ensuring coherence between IIAs and other areas of public policy, including policies to address global challenges such as the protection of the environment (climate change) or public health and safety. Finally, the underlying dynamics of IIA rulemaking have changed. A rise in South–South FDI flows and emerging economies' growing role as outward investors – also vis-à-vis the developed world – are beginning to alter the context and background against which IIAs are being negotiated.

It is the purpose of the *sequels* to consider how the issues described in the first-generation Pink Series have evolved, particularly focusing on treaty practice and the process of arbitral interpretation. Each of the *sequels* will have similar key elements, including (a) an introduction explaining the issue in today's broader context; (b) a stocktaking of IIA practice and arbitral awards; and (c) a section on policy options for IIA negotiators, offering language for possible new clauses that better take into account the development needs of host countries and enhance the stability and predictability of the legal system.

The updates are conceptualized as *sequels*, i.e. they aim to complement rather than replace the first-generation Pink Series. Compared to the first generation, the *sequels* will offer a greater level of detail and move beyond a merely informative role. In line with UNCTAD's mandate, they will aim at analysing the development impact and strengthening the development dimension of IIAs. The *sequels* are finalized through a rigorous process of peer reviews, which benefits from collective learning and sharing of experiences. Attention is placed on ensuring involvement of a broad set of stakeholders, aiming to capture ideas and concerns from society at large.

The *sequels* are edited by Anna Joubin-Bret, and produced by a team under the direction of Jörg Weber and the overall guidance of James Zhan. The members of the team include Wolfgang Alschner, Bekele Amare, Hamed El-Kady, Jan Knörich, Sergey Ripinsky, Claudia Salgado, Ileana Tejada and Elisabeth Tuerk.

This paper is based on a study prepared by Peter Muchlinski. Anna Joubin-Bret and Sergey Ripinsky finalized the paper. Comments were received from Sedat Çal, Vilawan Mangklatanakul, Julie A. Maupin and Khondaker Golam Moazzem. The paper also benefited from comments made at an ad-hoc expert group meeting convened by UNCTAD in December 2009 on "Key issues in the evolving system of international investment rule-making", which was attended by numerous experts and practitioners in this field.

Supachai Panitchpakdi
Secretary-General of UNCTAD

January 2011

CONTENTS

FIGURES

BOXES

ABBREVIATIONS

ASEAN	Association of South-East Asian Nations
BIT	bilateral investment treaty
CARICOM	Caribbean Community
CARIFORUM	Caribbean Forum
COMESA	Common Market for Eastern and Southern Africa
ECT	Energy Charter Treaty
EPA	economic partnership agreement
EU	European Union
FDI	foreign direct investment
FTA	free trade agreement
GATS	General Agreement on Trade in Services
ICJ	International Court of Justice
ICSID	International Centre for Settlement of Investment Disputes
IIA	international investment agreement
IMF	International Monetary Fund
IPR	intellectual property right
LDC	least developed country
NAFTA	North American Free Trade Agreement
OECD	Organisation for Economic Cooperation and Development
R&D	Research and development
SCC	Stockholm Chamber of Commerce
TNC	transnational corporation
UNCITRAL	United Nations Commission on International Trade Law
WTO	World Trade Organization

EXECUTIVE SUMMARY

This paper analyses the scope and definitions of international investment agreements (IIAs). IIAs must specify not only their geographical and temporal coverage, but, most importantly, their subject-matter coverage. This is done primarily through the definitions of the terms "investment" and "investor", which form the main focus of this paper. The definition of "investment" determines economic interests, to which governments extend substantive IIA protections, while the definition of "investor" specifies the range of individuals and legal entities that can benefit from the treaty.

To a large extent, the definitions outline the boundaries of a country's exposure to possible investor–State claims. The outcomes of many arbitral decisions of the past decade have depended on a tribunal's interpretation of whether a particular transaction or asset qualified as a protected investment and/or whether the claimant qualified as a protected investor. Arbitral decisions have revealed a wealth of implications that particular definitional approaches or particular treaty wording may have. Accordingly, the second edition of this paper not only considers how investment and investor been defined in existing investment agreements but also how different definitions are likely to be interpreted.

With respect to the definition of investment, while the broad and open-ended asset-based definition has remained wide-spread in BITs focusing on investment protection, newer agreements have used techniques for narrowing the scope of the definition. This trend is likely to have been a reaction to those arbitral awards which interpreted open-ended definitions in an over-extensive manner. In particular, some treaties started to use a closed-list definition instead of an open-ended one, introduce certain objective criteria or elements to determine when an asset can be considered an investment, explicitly exclude certain types of assets and employ other narrowing techniques. Arbitral practice has further highlighted the importance of a proviso that a treaty should apply only to those investments that are made in accordance with host State law.

An additional complication that has emerged with regard to the term "investment" is the interrelationship between its scope under the applicable IIA, on the one hand, and under Article 25(1) of the International Centre for Settlement of Investment (ICSID) Convention, on the other. Tribunals have differed as to which of the two should be treated as decisive as well as to the exact meaning of "investment" under the ICSID Convention, which requires the existence of an "investment" but does not define the term. An important question in this debate is whether an investment must contribute to the economic development of the host State in order for the ICSID Convention to apply.

With respect to the definition of investor, there are distinct issues concerning individuals and legal entities. The position of natural persons is generally less controversial, and the relevant questions center mostly on whether treaty coverage can – in addition to citizens of the home States – be extended to its permanent residents and/or dual nationals. The increased mobility of global population also means that the economic links of a person with the country of his/her citizenship may be weak or even non-existent, hence the issue of whether such person should be covered by a treaty.

The status of legal entities is more complicated. The nationality of a company can be determined using a number of tests, each having its advantages and disadvantages. The country-of-incorporation test remains prevalent in IIAs, even though its limitations have been exposed in several high-profile cases that have dealt with "treaty shopping" practices. Where an IIA employs the country-of-incorporation test as the sole criterion, the issue has arisen whether an arbitral tribunal must "pierce the corporate veil" in order to identify the nationality of the company's ultimate owners or controllers. Most arbitral tribunals have decided that the country-of-incorporation test does not authorize or require them to do so.

This issue needs to be given due attention, if a State wishes to eliminate the risk of claims by "mailbox" companies. There has been an increasing trend to combine the formal country-of-incorporation test with a requirement that a company have its seat in the same country and/or carry out real economic activities there. Another alternative is to supplement the country-of-incorporation test with a denial-of-benefits clause, even though early arbitral practice has demonstrated that a discretionary denial-of-benefits clause may be not as effective in practice as generally believed. Finally, there is a possibility to determine the nationality of an investor by reference to the nationality of individuals who ultimately own or control it. Prone to practical difficulties, this method would, however, allow "piercing the corporate veil" in order to determine the "true" nationality of the company. The country-of-incorporation test will suffice, however, if a State is willing to grant IIA protection to investments regardless of the nationality of persons who ultimately own or control them. In the context of definitional clauses, negotiators have to further consider issues of multiple claims and claims by minority shareholders.

It has to be remembered that there is no such thing as the best definition of "investment" or "investor"; they are simply a reflection of each country's preferences and policies. This paper discerns the implications of particular treaty approaches and wording in order to assist States in finding a formula that would suit their policy objectives.

Furthermore, it is obvious that the definitions alone cannot establish an appropriate balance between affording a sufficient degree of protection to foreign investors and preserving the vital interests of the host country, including its regulatory policy space. This fundamental goal needs to be kept in mind when drafting both the definitions and each individual substantive obligation of the investment agreement.

INTRODUCTION

This paper is the first of a series of revised editions of the UNCTAD Series on *Issues in International Investment Agreements* (IIAs). It is the purpose of this paper to consider how the issue of scope and definition has evolved, both in treaty practice and in the process of arbitral interpretation. The universe of IIAs has grown dramatically since the publication of the first edition of this paper in 1999. During 2008, the network of IIAs continued to expand, although the number of bilateral investment treaties (BITs) concluded in 2008 (59) was lower than in 2007 (65). The total number of BITs rose to 2,750 at the end of 2009 (UNCTAD 2010, p. 81). Equally, the impact of IIAs has developed and changed. In their inception, during the period of post-World War II decolonization, IIAs were negotiated to have broad coverage and protect against many potential threats. In particular, the threat of mass expropriation in the course of strategic national economic plans was seen as a major problem for investors in newly independent host countries that had been former colonies of the major powers. On the other hand, IIAs had rather limited dispute settlement provisions that were centered on State-to-State mechanisms. However, since the adoption, in 1965, of the Washington Convention on the Settlement of Investment Disputes between States and Nationals of other States (ICSID Convention) this has changed and IIAs, especially BITs, routinely have an investor–State dispute settlement clause. In such clauses, recourse to ICSID is often provided as the main arbitration forum.

Until recently, such forms of dispute settlement were relatively uncommon. But since the beginning of the twenty-first century, investor–State dispute settlement cases have increased at an unprecedented rate.[1] As a result, an extensive arbitral interpretation of specific clauses in IIAs has arisen, including scope and definition clauses. This is referred to sometimes as "case-law", though the more appropriate description is "arbitral interpretation", as awards of tribunals in this field are not binding on third parties to the dispute and there is no doctrine of precedent that requires subsequent tribunals to follow the reasoning of earlier awards. That said, the outcomes of awards and the reasons for them cannot be ignored in any contemporary discussion of IIA clauses.

The arbitral interpretation process has created a new learning environment for countries and, in particular, for IIA negotiators. Countries and negotiators are learning from their experiences and new challenges lie ahead as the first generation of treaties comes up for renewal and renegotiation. Specifically, given the kinds of interpretations the scope and definition clauses have had in recent years, concern has grown over the actual coverage of IIAs and whether they are offering too wide a field of support for investors and the various categories of investments that specific treaties have been found to protect. The risk to the policy space of the host country is enhanced in this way, as transactions that were not thought to be investments at the time of the agreement's signature might suddenly become covered. For example, in recent arbitral awards, as will be seen below, certain types of contractual claims have now been regarded as "investments" under IIA provisions and so are capable of being the subject of a claim before an arbitral panel. A number of other phenomena that may appear undesirable to States have emerged, such as structuring of investments by domestic investors through foreign companies to avail themselves of the IIA protection; other forms of treaty shopping; risk of multiple claims brought by various links in the corporate chain under different IIAs; and others.

Such concerns result in a changing environment for negotiators and a change in negotiating objectives. In particular, it is now open to discussion whether IIAs have become too one-sided in that expansive interpretations of the scope of coverage and protection offered by such agreements have led to fears that the host country's national policy space and right to regulate have been unduly curtailed in ways that might adversely affect genuine development policy objectives (UNCTAD 2003, chapters V and VI). In addition, given the emphasis placed by host countries on investor and investment promotion, it may be useful for protection to be more targeted covering not all investments, but only investments that can contribute to development.

In the light of such concerns, the negotiator's objective today may be to ensure that the treaty covers those investors/investments that can further development objectives. Such objectives have themselves changed over time since the first BITs were negotiated. In particular, although still very significant, no longer is the major capital-intensive natural resource extraction or infrastructure development project the main type of development-oriented investment project covered by the agreement. In more recent years, the emphasis has shifted to a larger number of small- and medium-sized projects aimed towards export-oriented manufacturing, services provision and R&D development in the developing host country (UNCTAD 2002; 2004; and 2005a). This entails two objectives in particular. First, IIAs should be focused on investment that generates development benefits and, secondly, that the stability and predictability of the legal system, required by investors and their investments, is enhanced by clear and focused rules. This is particularly important in the context of investment liberalization agreements with rights of entry and establishment. Here the definition of protected investors and investments needs to be confined to what really needs to be covered so as to ensure a balance of protection rights for investors and investments and legitimate rights of regulation for host countries. Equally, there are awards that stress the need to consider the development dimension in determining the protected subject matter of an IIA. The analysis contained in these awards is of value to the evolution of a genuine development-friendly new generation scope and definition clause.

Accordingly, these awards, and awards critical of this perspective, will be considered in detail in Section II below. Before that is done, Section I will provide an overview of the specific issues arising in the context of scope and definition clauses. Finally, Section III will put forward certain policy options for future agreements and will offer examples of possible new model clauses that take more fully into account the development needs of host countries.

Note

[1]   For recent figures on investor–State arbitrations, see UNCTAD 2010, p. 83.

I. EXPLANATION OF THE ISSUE

A. Scope of international investment agreements

In relation to treaty practice, the most-used definition of investment remains the broad asset-based definition of "investment" and the nationality-based definition of "investor". As will be seen below, both terms have been extensively interpreted in arbitral awards and this has given rise to concerns about the breadth of coverage of each term.

As a result, a further trend has been the increasing experimentation in newer agreements with techniques for narrowing the scope of these broad interpretations. In relation to "investor", these focus on nationality, ownership, control and in the case of legal persons, company seat and requirement of real economic activities in the home country (though many agreements still rely on a formal incorporation test). In the case of investments, narrowing techniques include:

- Applying the protection of the treaty only to investments made in accordance with host country law;

- Using a closed-list definition instead of an open-ended one;

- Excluding of portfolio shares by restricting the asset-based approach to direct investment only;

- Introducing investment risk and other objective factors to determine when an asset should be protected under the treaty;

- Excluding certain types of assets such as certain commercial contracts, certain loans and debt securities and assets used for non-business purposes;

- A more selective approach to intellectual property rights as protected assets; and

- Dealing with the special problems of defining the investment in the case of complex group enterprises as investors.

In addition to the key terms of "investor" and "investment", which define the coverage of protected persons and assets under the IIA, there are at least two further dimensions to the scope of an investment agreement, namely, the geographical and temporal scope. These are not usually determined by means of definitions, but through specific provisions, whether among the instrument's "final clauses" or in special provisions. The *geographical* scope of an investment agreement is determined, to begin with, by the number and identity of the States that are party to it. It is also determined by the territorial limits of the States concerned. The definition of the term "territory" is important in this respect and will be briefly addressed in Section II.C. To ascertain the exact *temporal* scope of an agreement, its date of entry into force with respect to each party and its duration has to be determined. Apart from such general international law questions, the temporal scope of an agreement raises the issue of whether the agreement applies to an investment established prior to its entry into force; this is often addressed in the definition of "investment" and will be discussed in connection with that term. Another issue is whether the provisions of an agreement continue to apply to established investments subsequent to the treaty's formal termination. Generally, this issue is not addressed in provisions on definitions and will not be discussed here.

States can further circumscribe the scope of IIAs by excluding certain matters such as taxation, government procurement or subsidies and grants, or by adding exceptions or reservations, etc. These issues are not discussed here and are left for consideration in other UNCTAD publications. This paper primarily addresses the problems of definitions, and especially those of the terms "investment" and "investor", around which cluster most of the important questions and whose importance has been highlighted by international arbitration.

B. Definitions of key terms

Definitions serve many purposes. In international agreements, they raise difficult policy issues and are often the subject of hard bargaining between the negotiating parties. Accordingly, they should be seen not as objective formulations of the meaning of terms, but as part of an agreement's normative content, since they determine the extent and the manner in which the other provisions are to be applied. Thus, the decision on a definition of terms will be made on a case-by-case basis, taking into account the purpose and circumstances of the negotiations at stake. In addition, the Vienna Convention on the Law of Treaties requires that tribunals look first to the ordinary meaning of the terms of the treaty as the best manifestation of negotiators intent, and that, as a rule, the specific, substantive provisions of a treaty are given priority over generalized principles such as those contained in preambles.[1] Therefore, negotiators need to make their intentions manifest in the specific provisions, including definitions.

In relation to scope and definition clauses the foregoing considerations raise the question of how best to define the terms "investment" and "investor" in the light of overarching priorities and development concerns.

1. Definition of investment

(i) Historical development of the concept

The conception of what constitutes foreign investment has changed over time as the nature of international economic relations has changed. The development of the types of assets that could be the subject of protection under international investment agreements has widened significantly since the mid-nineteenth century. Prior to that time, trans-frontier capital flows typically assumed the form of lending by European investors to borrowers in other European States (Kindleberger 1993, pp. 208-224). Foreign direct investment (FDI) was not as such the main form of international investment. Rather, foreign-owned property in a country often took the form of tangible property and financial interests in investments. International law was thus concerned principally with the protection of such property against seizure and the right of creditors to collect debts. Some countries negotiated treaties that protected foreign property, such as merchandise and vessels, against expropriation.[2]

By the mid-twentieth century, the protection of foreign investment in the form of equity stock in companies became an increasing concern of international law. Since much FDI was in the primary sector, concession agreements for natural resource extraction became a matter of importance in international law.[3] By the late twentieth century, the forms of foreign investment became more diverse. As technological innovations spread around the world, the producers of technology sought to protect their patents and copyrighted materials against infringement. The consolidation of business enterprises to form transnational corporations (TNCs) with global name recognition has given great value to certain trademarks that are associated with high quality and/or high demand goods. Thus, the regulation of intellectual property has become a concern of growing importance to national and international law. Many developed economies that had concentrated their productive resources in the manufacturing sector in the nineteenth century began to shift a large portion of these resources to the services sector, and continuing improvements in communication and transportation made it feasible for service providers to render services to clients in foreign countries (UNCTAD 2004). As this suggests, changing circumstances create new ways of investment in foreign countries. In other words, there is an increasing array of foreign-owned assets that have economic value and thus may be regarded as foreign investment.

(ii) Need for increased precision

This creates the potential for investment to become an open-ended and vague term in IIAs. Clear benchmarks as to what is an investment must be developed so as to assess whether a given asset or transaction is an investment or some other kind of uncovered commercial transaction. These benchmarks will form the basis of treaty text that may subsequently be interpreted on a case-by-case basis in an arbitral award. Where it is clear that the IIA in question sets limits as to what can be regarded as an investment under the terms of the agreement, a tribunal must respect those limitations. Thus, in the negotiating process, it is now important to consider how to send a clear message as to the mutually agreed limits of protected investments under the IIA.

The continued domination of the traditional broad asset-based definition risks the possibility that transactions that were not thought to be investments at the time the agreement was entered into might nonetheless become covered as a result of an open-ended nature of the definition. An issue of contractual claims has arisen in this regard and, in particular, the question of the distinction between an ordinary commercial transaction and an investment. Many IIAs containing a broad asset-based definition include *"claims to money and claims under a contract having a financial value"*. This category may be taken as suggesting that the term "investment" encompasses even ordinary commercial transactions unless the latter are specifically excluded. The language does not seem to require that the contracts be long-term contracts. As written, it does not appear to distinguish between transactions that might be regarded as trade in services and those that might be regarded as investment in services. In the light of such broad provisions, there is a danger of a gradual extension, by arbitral tribunals, of the types of contractual claims that can be regarded as assets capable of protection under the broad asset-based definition of investment.

(iii) Narrowing the definition

Because of the risk of an overbroad interpretation of what constitutes investment, various restrictions on a wide approach can be introduced into the scope and definition clause. In the first place, certain specific assets could be excluded from the definition. For example, portfolio shares can be excluded from the definition of covered assets. One reason for this possibility is that the risk involved in some portfolio investments for the investor would not be as high as that involved in a direct investment, since the former investment could normally be pulled out of a host country more easily than the latter (Sornarajah 2004, pp. 227-228). Other approaches can restrict protection only to direct investments or investments made though a locally established enterprise, thereby emphasizing that only a contribution based on a transfer of finance and managerial control over the investment will be sufficient to warrant protection, given the greater commitment of resources and risk that this entails on the part of the investor. In more recent years, as noted in Section II below, the use of a tightly defined "closed list" of protected assets has also become the practice of some countries in their IIAs. This allows for a wide range of interests to be protected but with a clear set of defining characteristics allowing for a clearer distinction to be drawn between covered and uncovered assets and transactions.

An additional requirement is that only investments made in accordance with host country law could be given protection. In this way, investments that fail to abide by the law of the host country, as applied upon entry and establishment, will lose the protection of the IIA, as they do not qualify as protected investments due to their illegality. Depending on the exact formulation of the requirement, it could conceivably be used to deprive an investor of the treaty protection for serious violations of host country law admitted during the life of an investment, i.e. after it is made.

In is also possible to include objective criteria for the definition of an investment to be covered by the agreement, based on contribution of capital, investment risk, duration and contribution to development. Finally the problems created by an overbroad protection of intellectual property rights (IPRs) as investments need to be considered. Extending protection to those IPRs that are not protected under domestic law of a State may lead to an undue restriction of regulatory discretion in dealing with such rights in the context of the need for technology and skills transfer as part of its development policy. Accordingly, more focused and limited protection could be required through a more specific definition of protected IPRs.

(iv) The application of Article 25(1) of the ICSID Convention

In addition to these problems, a further difficulty emerges from the fact that many arbitrations are based on a BIT with an open-ended asset-based definition of "investment" and are at the same time brought before the International Centre for Settlement of Investment Disputes established under the ICSID Convention. The latter also uses the term "investment", without, however, defining it. Article 25(1) of the ICSID Convention, the pillar of ICSID jurisdiction, states:

> "[t]he jurisdiction of the Centre shall extend to any legal dispute **arising directly out of an investment**, between a Contracting State (or any constituent subdivision or agency of a Contracting State...) and a national of another Contracting State, which the

parties to the dispute consent in writing to submit to the Centre." (Emphasis added.)

As will be discussed fully in Section II.A.(4), arbitral tribunals have differed as to whether the definition of investment given in the BIT or an interpretation of "investment" under Article 25(1) of the ICSID Convention is decisive. This has significant implications for a development-oriented approach to defining the term. Certain tribunals have interpreted the term "investment" in Article 25(1) as connoting certain objective features that characterize any investment as well as certain development-related impacts, even though these elements are not expressly mentioned in Article 25. Under this approach, the term "investment" under the ICSID Convention can turn out to be narrower that the same term in the applicable IIA, especially if the latter uses a broad asset-based definition. Other tribunals have held that the definition found in the applicable IIA should be a controlling one. The question remains which approach should prevail. From a development perspective, the former would appear preferable and, given the importance of ICSID as a centre for investor–State arbitration under IIAs, it would seem reasonable to suggest that the ICSID Convention determines subject-matter jurisdiction rather than the individual BIT given the choice of the parties to take the dispute to ICSID. On the other hand such a perspective could encourage investors to go to ad hoc arbitration based on the BIT alone rather than to ICSID.

(v) The impact of complex corporate group structures

Finally, mention must be made of the special problems arising in the case of complex group enterprises as investors. Broad definitions of investment recognize both direct and indirect shareholding as protected assets which can lead to multiple claims. That is, a parent company can structure its investment in the host State through one or more intermediate holding companies established in various countries. Each of these companies will potentially have a right to bring a claim, provided that the relevant country has an IIA with the host State. Claims made by intermediate holding companies arising out of their investments in subsidiaries are not uncommon. They are seen by tribunals as within the jurisdiction of BITs containing references to interests in companies as a category of protected investment (Dolzer and Schreuer 2008, pp. 54–55). This has led to the use of holding or shell companies, incorporated in jurisdictions enjoying investment treaty relations with host countries, as a means of enhancing protection under IIAs, especially where the home country of the parent company has no treaty in place with a given host country. This practice is often referred to as "treaty shopping". The implications of this situation will be further considered in Section II.A.(5).

The reference to interests in companies typically does not require that the investor's interest or participation in the company be a controlling one. Indeed, minority shareholdings are generally protected under IIAs and arbitral tribunals have supported this approach (McLachlan et al. 2007, pp. 187–189).

2. Definition of investor

Investment agreements generally apply only to investment by those who qualify as covered investors according to the agreement's provisions. The definition of the term "investor" thus can be critical to determining the scope of an investment agreement. Two general issues arise in defining the term "investor": what types of person or entity may be considered investors, and what are the criteria that determine that a person is covered by an agreement? Two types of person may be included within the definition of "investor": natural persons or individuals and legal persons, also referred to as legal or juridical entities. Sometimes, the term "investor" is not used. Instead, agreements refer to "nationals" and "companies", with the former defined to include natural persons and the latter defined to include a range of legal entities.[4]

(i) Natural persons

In relation to the category of natural persons, the major issue concerns the determination of whether a natural person is covered by an agreement. This is based on the qualifying links of the person with the State party to the agreement. Typically, this is a nationality link but other links, such as permanent residence, domicile, residence or combinations thereof are also in use. For natural persons, the criteria for determining nationality in the IIA usually refer to the relevant national laws of the Contracting parties for the determination of nationality (Schlemmer 2008, pp. 69–70). Normally, this raises few problems in practice. In most cases, the individual investor seeking protection under the IIA is the national of another State Party. However, in cases of dual nationality, as will be noted fully in Section II.B.(1), arbitral awards have so far refused to apply the general principle found in international law based on the effective link test, so far as personal jurisdiction for the purposes of ICSID arbitration is concerned. Under customary international law, a State can exercise diplomatic protection on behalf of one of its nationals with respect to a claim against another State, even if its national also possesses the nationality of the other State, provided that the dominant and effective nationality of the person was of the State exercising diplomatic protection (cf. *Nottebohm Case* and *Barcelona Traction Case*).[5] Typically, this test is not found in existing investment agreements, which tend to be silent on the matter of dual nationality. Whether this situation is supportable in practice will be considered further in Section II.B.(1)(c).

(ii) Legal entities

The category of legal entities, by contrast, can be defined to include or exclude a number of different types of entities. Entities may be excluded on the basis of their legal form, their purpose or their ownership. Differences in the legal form of an entity may be important to a host country in a variety of circumstances. The form of the entity determines, for example, which assets may be reached by creditors of the entity to satisfy debts and perhaps the extent to which the entity can be sued in its own name in the courts. A host country may wish to exclude from the category of covered investors State-owned entities such as sovereign wealth funds or those entities that, because of legal limitations on liability or susceptibility to suit, are insulated from financial responsibility for any injuries that they may cause. In addition, the host country may require that the entity have real and effective commercial links with the home country party to the relevant IIA. In this way, only investors from that contracting party will have the right to protection under the agreement.

Indeed, corporate nationality may raise questions of its misuse, especially in the context of transnational corporate group structures. For example, nationals of one contracting party to an IIA may incorporate an entity in the other contracting party, so as to take advantage of the IIA rules against their own country (figure 1). Arguably, this is incompatible with the actual intent of the IIA, which is to give protection to foreign investors from another contracting party and not to domestic investors operating through a foreign "shell" company. Equally, investors from a country that is not a party to any IIAs with the host country may incorporate an entity in a third country to take advantage of its IIA with the host country. This is known as "treaty shopping" and it too raises questions as to the proper approach to defining corporate investors for the purposes of an IIA. These two situations raise the question whether the IIA should authorize an arbitral tribunal to "lift the corporate veil" to reach the actual controlling interests and to determine whether they qualify, by reason of nationality, as proper parties to the claim made under the IIA in question. Such arrangements have caused controversy in arbitral awards as will be seen in Section II.B.(2)(b).

Figure 1. Indirect investment with the parent company originating from the host State

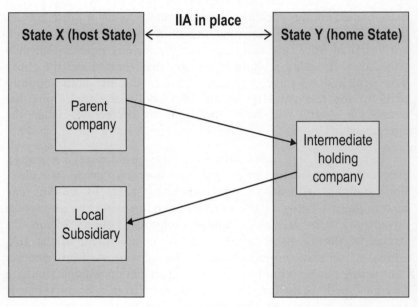

A further problem arising out of complex corporate group structures is whether an indirect controlling interest that possesses the nationality of a contracting party can still make a claim on behalf of an indirectly owned affiliate where its direct owner is located in a non-contracting party. The specific problem here is whether a company indirectly owned or controlled by another comes within the scope of an agreement. For example, where company "A" has a controlling interest in company "B" that has a controlling interest in company "C", does that make company "C" an investment controlled by company "A" as well as company "B" (figure 2)? This has particular repercussions where not every country in which the companies operate is a party to an agreement. Thus, to return to the example, should company "B" have the nationality of a country not party to the agreement, while companies "A" and "C" have the nationality of countries party to the agreement, can company "A" still claim the protection of the agreement despite the fact that its investment in "C" is channeled through "B", i.e. through a non-party? Arbitral awards have on the whole been sympathetic to accepting jurisdiction over such indirect claims as will be discussed in Section II.B.(2)(b). This raises the question of how IIAs should address the issue, especially given the proliferation of integrated international production systems established by TNCs.

Figure 2. Indirect investment structured through a third State which does not have an IIA with the host State

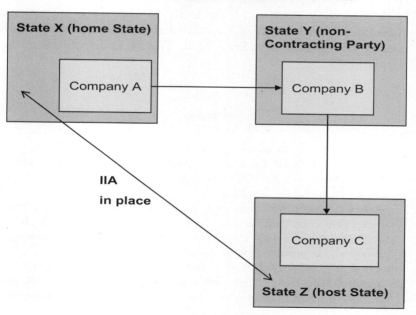

(iii) Denial of benefits

In policy terms, the issue of establishing the nationality of an investor presents the question of the extent to which the parties to an agreement wish to link the legal coverage of the agreement with the economic ties between the parties and the covered investment. One country may be seeking to establish a generally favourable investment climate and may be prepared to extend treaty coverage to investments that have minimal economic ties with the other party, while another country may wish to extend treaty coverage only to investments with strong economic ties to the treaty partners. Thus, IIAs have included "denial of benefits" clauses to restrict the benefit of the agreement only to investors who possess that nationality of a contracting party. Pursuant to a denial-of-benefits clause, a host State may deny benefits of the treaty to "letterbox" companies constituted in the territory of the other party by persons from a third country or from the host State itself. This is further discussed in Section II.B.(2)(d).

Notes

[1]　See Vienna Convention on the Law of Treaties (1969), Articles 31-32.

[2]　See, e.g., Article 10, General Convention of Peace, Amity, Navigation and Commerce, United States-Colombia, 3 October 1824 in United States Treaty Series, No. 52.

[3]　See, e.g., *Petroleum Development Limited v. Sheikh of Abu Dhabi*, Judgement (*International Law Reports*, 1951, Vol. 18, pp. 144-164); *Sapphire International Petroleum Limited v. National Iranian Oil Company*, Judgement (*International Law Reports*, 1967, Vol. 27, pp. 117-233); *Ruler of Qatar v. International Marine Oil Company Limited*, Judgement (*International Law Reports*, 1953, Vol. 20, pp. 534-547); *Saudi Arabia v. Arabian American Oil Company*

(ARAMCO), Judgement (*International Law Reports*, 1963, Vol. 27, pp. 117-233).

[4] In addition, certain instruments refer specifically to "transnational corporations" or to "multinational enterprises". These terms tend to appear in institutional policy-oriented documents such as the Organisation for Economic Co-operation and Development (OECD) Guidelines for Multinational Enterprises or the Draft United Nations Code of Conduct on Transnational Corporations. These terms are not generally used in IIAs and so need not be further considered in this paper. For a full discussion of the relationship between these terms, see Muchlinski 2007, pp. 6–7. For a deeper discussion see UNCTAD 1999, pp. 45–48.

[5] *Nottebohm Case (Liechtenstein v. Guatemala)*, ICJ, Judgement, 18 November 1953; Judgement, 6 April 1955 (*ICJ Reports*, 1955, pp. 4-65); *Barcelona Traction, Light and Power Company, Limited (Belgium v. Spain)*, ICJ, 1970, Judgement, 24 July 1964; Judgement, 5 February 1970 (*ICJ Reports*, 1970, pp. 3-357).

II. STOCKTAKING AND ANALYSIS

This section shall cover the main developments in both treaty and arbitral practice that have arisen since the publication of the first edition of this paper. Since that time, a significant number of investor–State disputes have been determined. While it would be beyond the scope of this paper to cover every case in which the terms "investment" or "investor" have been discussed, it aims to highlight the main trends of analysis found in selected leading arbitral awards. These are not always clear or consistent and so a simple description of decisions is insufficient. The approach will be to consider awards from the perspective of how far the interpretation given therein is conducive to achieving flexibility for development in IIAs, for the ensuring of a proper balance between the protection of investor and investment rights and the host country's right to regulate in the furtherance of legitimate public and developmental interests, as well as in relation to the creation of a clear definitional structure.

A. Investment

1. Main types of definitions

Traditionally, IIAs have used asset-based definitions in investor/investment protection agreements. Protection-oriented instruments seek to safeguard the interests of the investors or, in broader context, to promote foreign investment by safeguarding the investors' property rights, assets and interests. Investment is seen as something that already exists or that will exist, by the time protection becomes necessary. The older terminologies, which referred to "acquired rights" or to "foreign property" (OECD Draft Convention on the Protection of Foreign Property 1962) make the context clear. The exact character of the particular assets is not by itself important in this case, since protection is to be extended to assets after their acquisition by the investor, when they form part of the investor's patrimony.

Instruments mainly directed at the protection of foreign investment contain definitions of investment that are generally broad and comprehensive. They cover not only the capital (or the resources) that has crossed borders with a view towards the creation of an enterprise or the acquisition of control over an existing one, but also most other kinds of assets of the enterprise or of the investor, such as property and property rights of various kinds, non-equity investment, including several types of loans and portfolio transactions, as well as other contractual rights, including sometimes rights created by administrative action of a host State (licenses, permits, etc.). Such a definition is very common in BITs.

Enterprise-based definition. On the other hand, some IIAs have opted for an enterprise-based definition pioneered by the Canada–United States Free Trade Agreement (FTA) (1988). That agreement defined investment as including the establishment or acquisition of a business enterprise, as well as a share in a business enterprise which provides the investor control over the enterprise. It also limited investment to enterprises that were a direct investment and thus excluded portfolio investment. The Canada-United States FTA (1988) has since been superseded by the North American Free Trade Agreement (NAFTA) (1992), which also employs an enterprise-based definition albeit a much broader (open-ended) one. The NAFTA definition designates an "enterprise" owned or controlled by an investor as a type of investment as well as lists more traditional types of assets including those linked to the activities of an enterprise such as equity or debt security of an enterprise. Also in contrast to the Canada-United States FTA, the NAFTA definition includes portfolio investment.

An enterprise-based approach is useful where the agreement covers pre-entry treatment as well as post-entry treatment, as the act of entry and establishment has to take place through a specific entity rather than through the mere transfer of assets such as goods and/or services. By contrast, a post-entry-only agreement stresses the protection of foreign-owned and controlled assets which do not take the form of an organized enterprise. Further, host States' laws and regulations are often addressed to enterprises (as opposed to their shareholders), so where an enterprise constitutes a type of investment, it becomes easier for such laws and regulations to be caught by the term "treatment of investments" used in various IIA obligations. Finally, by contrast to other types of investment, an "enterprise" has legal personality: treaties with enterprise-based approach often expressly enable a foreign investor to bring claims not only on its own behalf but also on behalf of its enterprise, which may have implications in terms of the amount of recoverable damages.

Definition by reference to "commercial presence". In some IIAs, covered investments are limited to those that take the form of "commercial presence", i.e. to legal entities established by an investor in the host State and branches or representative offices.[1] This type of definition is not used in classical investment protection treaties, however. Being very narrow in scope,[2] it is most often taken in agreements that have a specific aim of liberalizing trade in services. In these treaties, "commercial presence" is seen as one mode of cross-border supply of a service. Since it implies establishing a presence in a host State, it is also a form of FDI, and thus such agreements form part of the IIA universe. Treaties that employ the "commercial presence" definition do not include substantive protections of established investments (such as fair and equitable treatment, protection against expropriation, etc). Instead, they focus solely on providing market access opportunities.[3]

The European Union's (EU's) economic agreements take the concept of "commercial presence" beyond services and apply it to a broader range of economic activities. In terms of substantive obligations, however, they are similar to services agreements and are limited to liberalization.[4] Thus, the "commercial presence" definition serves the purposes of liberalization/market access agreements but is too narrow for investment protection treaties which usually seek to protect a much broader range of assets.[5]

2. The broad asset-based definition of investment

As already noted, the broad asset-based definition is dominant in the vast majority of IIAs and BITs and has been subject of significant arbitral interpretation. It states, initially, that investment includes "every kind of asset", suggesting that the term embraces everything of economic value, virtually without limitation. Some BITs include the language "every kind of economic interest", which begs a distinction between "asset" and "interest" and is likely even broader. The general definition is followed by an illustrative list of the main categories of investment to be protected. Typically these categories will cover:

- Movable and immovable property and any other property rights such as mortgages, liens and pledges;

- Shares, stocks and debentures of companies or interests in the property of such companies;

- Claims to money or to any performance under contract having a financial value;

- Intellectual property rights and goodwill; and

- Business concessions conferred by law or under contract, including concessions to search for, cultivate, extract or exploit natural resources.

These categories are expressly included within the definition of "investment", but the listing is not exhaustive. Accordingly, assets of "every kind" are included, even if they do not fall under the five categories. These categories are typical of those that appear in investment agreements with broad definitions of "investment" (see box 1).[6]

Box 1. Selected examples of broad asset-based definitions in IIAs

China–Pakistan FTA (2006)

Article 46 Definitions

For the purpose of this Chapter,

1. The term "investment" means every kind of asset invested by investors of one Party in accordance with the laws and regulations of the other Party in the territory of the latter, and particularly, though not exclusively, includes:

(a) movable and immovable property and other property rights such as mortgages, pledges and similar rights;

(b) shares, debentures, stock and any other kind of participation in companies;

(c) claims to money or to any other performance having an economic value associated with an investment;

(d) intellectual property rights, in particular copyrights, patents, trade-marks, trade-names, technical process, know-how and good-will;

(e) business concessions conferred by law or under contract permitted by law, including concessions to search for, cultivate, extract or exploit natural resources.

/...

Box 1 (continued)

Azerbaijan-Finland BIT (2003)

Article 1

Definitions

The term 'Investment' means every kind of asset established or acquired by an investor of one Contracting Party in the territory of the other Contracting Party in accordance with the laws and regulations of the latter Contracting Party including, in particular, though not exclusively:

(a) movable and immovable property or any property rights such as mortgages, liens, pledges, leases, usufruct and similar rights;

(b) shares, stocks, debentures or other form of participation in a company;

(c) titles or claims to money or rights to performance having an economic value;

(d) intellectual property rights, such as patents, copyrights, technical processes, trade marks, industrial designs, business names, know-how and goodwill; and

(e) concessions conferred by law, by administrative act or under a contract by a competent authority, including concessions to search for, develop, extract or exploit natural resources.

Any alteration of the form in which assets are invested or reinvested does not affect their character as investments.

/...

Box 1 (concluded)

Botswana–Ghana BIT (2003)

Article 1

Definitions

1. For the purpose of this Agreement:

(a) 'Investments' means every kind of asset and in particular, though not exclusively, includes:

(i) Movable and immovable property and any other property rights such as mortgages, liens or pledges;

(ii) Shares in and stocks and debentures of a company and any other form of participation in a company

(iii) Claims to money or to any performance under contract having a financial value;

(iv) Intellectual property rights, goodwill, technical processes and know how;

(v) Business concessions conferred by law or under contract, including concessions to search for, cultivate, extract or exploit natural resources; [...]

Reinvestment. A further question is whether the term "investment" covers reinvestment, that is to say, the investment of the proceeds of the initial investment or whether only such reinvestment that is formally authorized is covered. Those proceeds have presumably been earned in the host country and have not been imported from abroad, as may have been the initial capital (or part of it). To the extent that national or international rules on foreign investment seek to encourage the importation of foreign capital, in whatever form, the reinvestment of earnings may be seen from the host country's point of view as not qualifying. On the other hand, foreign investors, in making investment decisions, will take into account a host country's policies regarding treatment of all their assets and are likely to prefer that they be treated in the same manner, whether purchased initially by imported capital or financed through subsequent reinvestment. For instance, the China–Finland BIT (2004) specifically provides in Article 1(1): *"Reinvested returns shall enjoy the same treatment as the original investment."*

Change in the form of investment. Many BITs provide that change in the form of investment is covered to the same extent as the original investment. For example, Article I of the United Kingdom–Mexico BIT (2006) provides that *"A change in the form in which assets are invested does not affect their character as investments as long as they are covered by this definition."*[7] This additional wording will have significance as and when foreign investors change the form of their original investment, for example from a claim under a contract into shares in a company. Investors will want to be able to restructure their investments without being concerned that they will no longer be protected by the relevant IIA. Some investment treaties state explicitly that reinvestment is covered only if established in accordance with the conditions placed on the initial investment. For example, Article 2 of the Belgium/Luxembourg–Cyprus BIT (1991) provides that *"[a]ny alteration of the form in which assets are invested shall not affect their classification as investment, provided that such alteration is not contrary to the approval, if any, granted in respect of the assets originally invested"*.

3. Narrowing the scope of the term "investment"

The possibility of taking a wide approach to the definition of investment may be contrasted with developments in recent treaty practice that seek to narrow down the scope of this term. A number of narrowing approaches need to be highlighted here:

- Excluding specific types of assets such as portfolio investments, certain commercial contracts, certain loans and debt securities, etc;

- Using a "closed list" definition with a wide asset-based list of examples which are exhaustive rather than illustrative;

- Limiting investments to those made "in accordance with host country law";

- Supplementing definitions of "investment" by express references to investment risk and other factors commonly associated with investment, thereby introducing objective criteria to the analysis of the term;

- Restricting covered investments depending on the time of their of establishment;

- Limiting covered investments to certain industry sectors;

- Restricting the range of covered intellectual property rights (IPRs).

(i) Exclusion of specific types of assets

Portfolio investments. Some investment agreements specify that they apply to foreign direct, as opposed to portfolio, investment. Portfolio investment is investment of a purely financial character, where the investor remains passive and does not control the management of the investment. The main concern of portfolio investors is the appreciation of the value of their capital and the return that it can generate, regardless of any long-term relationship consideration or control of the enterprise. Portfolio investment does not lead to technology transfer, training of local employees and other benefits associated with direct investment.

Where an agreement is limited to foreign direct investment, the covered investment must be more than a passive financial investment and must include in addition an element of management control over the investment. This limitation may be included in an agreement intended to facilitate international investment flows where the host country is seeking to attract foreign direct – but not necessarily foreign portfolio – investment, or where a host country is concerned about the possible detrimental effects of applying treaty provisions to certain types of investment, such as portfolio investment. For example, by Article 45 of the European Free Trade Association (EFTA)-Mexico FTA (2000):

"For the purpose of this Section, investment made in accordance with the laws and regulations of the Parties means direct investment, which is defined as investment for the purpose of establishing lasting economic relations with an undertaking such as, in particular, investments which give the possibility of exercising an effective influence on the management thereof."

Another example is the Framework Agreement on the Association of South-east Asian Nations (ASEAN) Investment Area (1998) which expressly excluded portfolio investments (Article 2).[8]

Governments may consider setting a benchmark, for example 10% of ordinary shares, to distinguish between direct and portfolio investments.[9] This approach would provide more certainty as to which investments are covered and which are not.

In addition to equity securities, the concept of portfolio investments also includes *debt securities* (IMF 1993, para. 385). Practically all IIAs have debt securities in the definition of investment, even though some IIAs choose to exclude debt securities with short original maturity (typically, less than three years) or to include in the definition only those debt securities whose original maturity exceeds a certain minimum time period. The usefulness of the distinction between long- and short-term debt securities is questionable as it is recognized that original maturity may have no bearing on the length of time that an investment will be held (ibid., para. 337).

Certain commercial contracts. The performance of a contract in a host country by a foreign entity may involve the creation of an investment and, as such, would be a natural element of a definition of investment. Indeed, contracts such as turnkey, construction, management, production, concession, revenue-sharing and other similar contracts are routinely included in a definition of investment. However, the fact that some IIAs also included *"claims to money and claims to any performance under contract having a financial value"*[10] has led some tribunals to recognize even ordinary one-off sales and services contracts as investments.

A number of countries have recognized that including ordinary commercial contracts in the definition of investment would lead to the term becoming overly broad and thus have started to add language specifically excluding such contracts from the definition of investment. Thus, Canada's model BIT (2004) provides in Article 1:

"but investment does not mean,

(X) claims to money that arise solely from

> *(i) commercial contracts for the sale of goods or services by a national or enterprise in the territory of a Party to an enterprise in the territory of the other Party [...]."*

Clauses of this type remove any doubt as to how contracts for sale of goods and services should be treated and provides helpful guidance to arbitral tribunals.

Certain loans and debt securities. Canada's model BIT (2004) also provides an example of a definition that excludes certain debt securities and loans:

- Debt securities and loans with the original maturity of less than three years (Article 1(III) and (IV);

- Debt securities of a State enterprise and loans to a State enterprise, regardless of their original maturity (Article 1(III) and (IV);

- A loan to or debt security issued by a financial institution which are not treated as regulatory capital by the Party in whose territory the financial institution is located;

- The extension of credit in connection with a commercial transaction, such as trade financing.

A different, less clear-cut example of this approach can be found in the Peru–United States FTA (2006). Article 10.28 sets out a definition of investment qualified by exclusions in footnotes. For example, while the definition covers *"bonds, debentures, other debt instruments and loans"*, a footnote in that Article states:

"Some forms of debt, such as bonds, debentures, and long-term notes, are more likely to have the characteristics of an investment, while other forms of debt, such as claims to payment that are immediately due and result from the sale of goods or services, are less likely to have such characteristics."

Public debt securities. Some States have chosen to exclude sovereign debt securities from covered investments,[11] as IIA obligations could interfere with debt restructuring or rescheduling in case of default or financial difficulties. Another option, employed in the Peru–United States FTA, is to limit an investor's ability to bring an investor–State claim based on a debt restructuring where holders of 75% or more of the outstanding debt have agreed to the restructuring.[12]

Assets used for non-business purposes. IIAs are typically aimed at promoting the flow of capital that would be used for business purposes. For this reason, a number of IIAs expressly exclude those foreign-owned assets that are intended for non-business use, such as vacation homes. IIAs do that in different ways:

- In a definition's chapeau: "*The term 'investment' shall mean every kind of asset **invested in connection with economic activities** by an investor of one Contracting Party…*" (Belarus–Czech Republic BIT (1996), Article 1, emphasis added);

- In the last "catch-all" sentence of the illustrative list of investments: "*interests arising from the commitment of capital or other resources in the territory of a Party **to economic activity in such territory**…*" (NAFTA (1992), Article 1139, emphasis added);

- In a separate note: "*For the purposes of this Chapter, 'loans and other forms of debt'* […] *and 'claims to money and claims to any other performance under contract'* […] ***refer to assets which relate to a business activity and do not refer to assets which are of personal nature, unrelated to any business activity***" (Japan–Singapore EPA (2002), Article 72(a), emphasis added).

An interesting facet of this requirement emerged in *Phoenix Action v. Czech Republic*, where the tribunal deprived the investment of the legal protection under the relevant BIT essentially because it found that the investment had been made with the sole aim of gaining access to the ICSID dispute settlement mechanism, rather than engaging in economic activity in the host State.[13] The tribunal held that such an investment violated a separate principle of good faith but its reasoning also suggests that for an investment to be eligible there must be a genuine intention to engage in an economic activity on the part of an investor.

(ii) "Closed list" approaches

The "closed list" approach illustrated by the definition of investment used in the Canadian model BIT of 2004 (box 2) differs from the broad open-ended approach in that it does not contain a conceptual chapeau to define investment (*"every kind of asset..."*) but contains an extensive but finite list of tangible and intangible assets to be covered by the treaty as well as certain clear exclusions of certain purely commercial transactions, including sales contracts and pure financial loan agreements involving no capital risk (UNCTAD 2007a, pp. 10-11). The "closed list" method can be applied to narrow down an asset-based definition as well as an enterprise-based definition.

Box 2. Scope of investment in the Canadian model BIT (2004)

"Investment means:
(I) an enterprise;
(II) an equity security of an enterprise;
(III) a debt security of an enterprise
(i) where the enterprise is an affiliate of the investor, or
(ii) where the original maturity of the debt security is at least three years,
but does not include a debt security, regardless of original maturity, of a state enterprise;
(IV) a loan to an enterprise
(i) where the enterprise is an affiliate of the investor, or
(ii) where the original maturity of the loan is at least three years,
but does not include a loan, regardless of original maturity, to a state enterprise;

/...

Box 2 (continued)

(V)   (i) notwithstanding subparagraph (III) and (IV) above, a loan to or debt security issued by a financial institution is an investment only where the loan or debt security is treated as regulatory capital by the Party in whose territory the financial institution is located, and

(ii) a loan granted by or debt security owned by a financial institution, other than a loan to or debt security of a financial institution referred to in (i), is not an investment;

for greater certainty:

(iii) a loan to, or debt security is sued by, a Party or a state enterprise thereof is not an investment; and

(iv) a loan granted by or debt security owned by a cross-border financial service provider, other than a loan to or debt security issued by a financial institution, is an investment if such loan or debt security meets the criteria for investments set out elsewhere in this Article;

(VI) an interest in an enterprise that entitles the owner to share in income or profits of the enterprise;

(VII) an interest in an enterprise that entitles the owner to share in the assets of that enterprise on dissolution, other than a debt security or a loan excluded from subparagraphs (III) (IV) or (V);

(VIII) real estate or other property, tangible or intangible, acquired in the expectation or used for the purpose of economic benefit or other business purposes; and

(IX) interests arising from the commitment of capital or other resources in the territory of a Party to economic activity in such territory, such as under

(i) contracts involving the presence of an investor's property in the territory of the Party, including turnkey or construction contracts, or concessions ,or

/...

Box 2 (concluded)

ii) contracts where remuneration depends substantially on the production, revenues or profits of an enterprise;
but investment does not mean,
(X) claims to money that arise solely from
(i) commercial contracts for the sale of goods or services by a national or enterprise in the territory of a Party to an enterprise in the territory of the other Party, or
(ii) the extension of credit in connection with a commercial transaction, such as trade financing, other than a loan covered by subparagraphs (IV) or (V); and

(XI) any other claims to money

that do not involve the kinds of interests set out in subparagraphs (I) through (IX). [Emphasis added]

(iii) Limitation to permitted investment under host country laws

Certain IIAs contain a specification that investment is covered only if made in accordance with the laws of the host country. For example, most of the BITs concluded by the People's Republic of China provide that "[t]*he term 'investment' means every kind of asset invested by investors of one Contracting Party in accordance with the laws and regulations of the other Contracting Party in the territory of the latter* ...".[14] This has the effect of making the protection of the investment under the BIT subject to the obtaining of any required approvals under the national laws of the host Contracting State party (Gallagher and Shan 2009, p. 56). Similarly, Article 1(9) of the Common Market for Eastern and Southern Africa (COMESA) Common Investment Area agreement (2007) states that "'*investment' means assets admitted or admissible in accordance with the relevant laws and regulations of the COMESA Member*

State in whose territory the investment is made". In agreements that apply this limitation, investment that is not established in accordance with the host country's laws and regulations will not be considered protected investment. One tribunal has emphasized that the relevant analysis *"has to be performed taking into account the laws in force at the moment of the establishment of the investment"* rather than later modifications in legislation.[15]

An alternative approach is to include a separate provision stating that an agreement shall apply only to investment made in accordance with the laws and regulations of the host country and/or previously approved by host State officials. Thus, in the new ASEAN Comprehensive Investment Agreement of 2009 the term "covered investment" means, with respect to a Member State, *"an investment in its territory of an investor of any other Member State in existence as of the date of entry into force of this Agreement or established, acquired or expanded thereafter, and has been admitted according to its laws, regulations, and national policies, and where applicable, specifically approved in writing by the competent authority of a Member State"*.

Particular attention is paid to this feature of investments, whether strictly in terms of definitions or otherwise, by agreements providing investment insurance or guarantees. For example, Article 15.6 of the Convention Establishing the Inter-Arab Investment Guarantee Corporation provides that *"[t]he conclusion of insurance contracts shall be subject to the condition that the investor shall have obtained the prior approval of the competent official authority in the host country for the making of the investment and for its insurance with the Corporation against the risks to be covered"*. And the Convention Establishing the Multilateral Investment Guarantee Agency, in Article 12 (d) on eligible investments provides that *"In guaranteeing an investment, the Agency shall satisfy itself as to: (ii) compliance of the investment with the host country's laws and regulations; (iii) consistency of the investment with the declared development objectives and priorities of the host country".*

Limiting the applicability of an investment agreement only to investments made in accordance with applicable laws and/or approval procedures is intended to induce foreign investors to ensure that all local laws and regulations are satisfied in the course of establishing an investment. This will have the additional effect of ensuring that both foreign and domestic investors are required to observe the laws of the land, thereby ensuring a "level playing field". Moreover, on the assumption that the host country's investment laws will be written and applied to further its development policy, this limitation also is intended to ensure that investment is covered only if it is consistent with the host country's development policy, and other policies, such as immigration or internal security, that impact on investment. Depending on the exact formulation of the requirement, it could conceivably be used to deprive an investor of the treaty protection for serious violations of host country law admitted during the life of an investment, i.e. after it is made.

Arbitral practice. Failure to comply with national laws and regulations could result in a tribunal refusing jurisdiction over any subsequent claim made by the investor.[16] Some tribunals have treated the requirement to comply with local laws as implicit even where not expressly stated in the relevant BIT.[17] There is also an emerging understanding that national legal systems include a general requirement of good faith that should prevent investments made through misrepresentations, concealments or corruption.[18]

However, the respondent country cannot rely on an interpretation of its national law that effectively excludes any recourse to remedies under the BIT. The overriding concern of good faith in the application of national investment approvals and other national regulatory requirements may be important in this connection. Thus, the withdrawal of an approval will not negate the fact that an investment has been made under applicable investment law. Otherwise, the host country could unilaterally undermine the protection of the applicable BIT (McLachlan et al. 2007, p. 196). Furthermore, as the tribunal in *Ioannis Kardassopoulos v. Georgia* observed, the State cannot preclude the protection of the BIT, *"on the ground that its own actions are illegal under its own laws. In other words, a host State cannot avoid jurisdiction under the BIT by invoking its own failure to comply with its domestic laws."*[19]

The need for good faith on the part of the host country has been recently reinforced by the decision of the tribunal in *Desert Line Projects LLC v. Yemen.*[20] The case arose out of a road construction project. The claimant had agreed to build a number of tarmac roads in Yemen. A dispute arose over payment to the claimant. The latter complained that the subsequent settlement of the dispute was inadequate and erroneous, and that its workers and personnel had been attacked and harassed by Yemeni personnel. On failure to resolve the dispute before the Yemeni courts, the claimant commenced proceedings before ICSID. The respondent State argued that the claimant's investment was not *"accepted, by the Host Party, as an investment according to its laws and regulations, and for which an investment certificate is issued"* as required by Article 1 of the Oman–Yemen BIT (1998). According to the respondent State, no such certificate had ever been issued and so the investment was not covered. The tribunal rejected this formal argument, saying that Article 1 should be interpreted as having a "material objective" and that this would not be served by a purely formal requirement that advanced no real interest of either signatory State but would, to the contrary, constitute, *"an artificial trap depriving investors of the very protection the BIT was intended to provide."*[21] On the facts, the investment had been accepted and welcomed by the Head of State in good faith and so the imposition of formalistic qualifications and requirements would have been offensive to *"the most elementary notions of good faith and insulting to the Head of State."*[22]

It should be noted that the reference to investments made in accordance with host country laws and procedures does not refer to definitions given by the laws and regulations of the host country but to the validity of the investment (Joubin-Bret 2008, p. 27). In effect it determines that only investments made in accordance with host country laws and regulations are to be given protection under the agreement. Illegal investments deserve no such protection.[23]

Whether the non-use of national law to define what constitutes an investment under an IIA should remain unaltered in future agreements is open to discussion. In particular, it is at least arguable that the definition of an investment covered by an IIA should take heed of any relevant definitions of an investment used in the national law of the host contracting party. This may be defended on the grounds that there appears to be an anomaly between the central role of national law in defining who may be seen as an "investor" under the IIA and its absence in relation to defining "investment". As will be shown below, the normal practice in relation to the definition of "investor" in IIAs is to refer to the nationality law of the home country of the investor and to see whether the candidate in question would qualify as a national under that law. If so, then they are a protected "investor". Yet in relation to "investment" national law plays no part in determining what this term means in the IIA. Accordingly, it may be that the national law of the host country should in future determine what is and is not a covered "investment" by reference to national law definitions. In this way, the agreement could further protect the regulatory space of the host country and ensure that only such investments are seen by host country law to fall into this category are protected under the IIA. The implications of such a provision will be further discussed in Section III.

(iv) Reference to investment risk and other factors

Another way to focus and control the scope of the term "investment" is to use an express reference to investment risk and other common economic features associated with an investment to provide objective criteria for a tribunal to assess whether the transaction before it is in fact a covered "investment". This approach may follow the features included in the so-called "Salini Test", which is further discussed in Section II.A.(4) in relation to Article 25 of the ICSID Convention, or it may use a narrower range of features. For example, the Colombian model BIT takes as its basis the similar test in the case of *Fedax v. Venezuela*[24] and, in Article 2.3 thereof lists these criteria as the minimum characteristics of an investment but leaves out the host State development criterion (Rivas 2009, p. 4).

An alternative approach, exemplified by United States BITs, is to limit the definition of investment to "*every asset that an investor owns or controls, directly or indirectly, that has the characteristics of an investment*" followed by an illustrative list of investments based on assets. In order to qualify as an investment under the United States model BIT (2004), an asset must have the characteristics of an investment, "*including such characteristics as the commitment of capital or other resources, the expectation of gain or profit, or the assumption of risk*" (box 3). Similarly, the Brunei–Japan EPA (2007) notes in the definition of investment that:

> "*Note 3: Where an asset lacks the characteristics of an investment, that asset is not an investment regardless of the form it may take. The characteristics of an investment include the commitment of capital, the expectation of gain or profit, or the assumption of risk.*"

One arbitral award stated that these three criteria constitute an "inherent common meaning" of the term "investment".[25] Similarly, a tribunal in *Romak v. Uzbekistan* held that *"the term 'investment' under the BIT has an inherent meaning entailing a contribution that extends over a certain period of time and that involves some risk."*[26] Accordingly, despite the broad definition of investment in the applicable BIT (*"every kind of assets and particularly..."*), the tribunal found that the claimant did not own an investment within the meaning of Article 1 of the BIT as its rights were embodied in and arose out of a sales contract. The tribunal, thus, dismissed the investor's claims for lack of jurisdiction.[27] However, this approach is not yet settled, and if a government wishes to make sure that objective characteristics of an investment be considered by a tribunal, it is well-advised to include them in the definition.

Box 3. Rwanda-United States BIT (2008)

Article 1

"Investment" means every asset that an investor owns or controls, directly or indirectly, that has the characteristics of an investment, including such characteristics as the commitment of capital or other resources, the expectation of gain or profit, or the assumption of risk. Forms that an investment may take include:

(a) an enterprise;1

(b) shares, stock, and other forms of equity participation in an enterprise;

(c) bonds, debentures, other debt instruments, and loans;2

(d) futures, options, and other derivatives;

(e) turnkey, construction, management, production, concession, revenue-sharing, and other similar contracts;

(f) intellectual property rights;

/...

Box 3 (concluded)

(g) licenses, authorizations, permits, and similar rights conferred pursuant to domestic law; 3, 4 and

(h) other tangible or intangible, movable or immovable property, and related property rights, such as leases, mortgages, liens, and pledges.

1. For greater certainty, where an enterprise does not have the characteristics of an investment, that enterprise is not an investment regardless of the form it may take.

2. Some forms of debt, such as bonds, debentures, and long-term notes, are more likely to have the characteristics of an investment, while other forms of debt, such as claims to payment that are immediately due and result from the sale of goods or services, are less likely to have such characteristics.

3. Whether a particular type of license, authorization, permit, or similar instrument (including a concession, to the extent that it has the nature of such an instrument) has the characteristics of an investment depends on such factors as the nature and extent of the rights that the holder has under the law of the Party. Among the licenses, authorizations, permits, and similar instruments that do not have the characteristics of an investment are those that do not create any rights protected under domestic law. For greater certainty, the foregoing is without prejudice to whether any asset associated with the license, authorization, permit, or similar instrument has the characteristics of an investment.

4. The term 'investment' does not include an order or judgment entered in a judicial or administrative action.

"Or" vs. "and". Importantly, many treaty provisions that set out characteristics of an investment operate with the conjunction "or", thereby emphasizing that not all factors need to exist for an investment to be identified (see, for example, the quotes from the treaties above). Thus an investment may be covered if it merely has "an expectation of profit" – it need not include a commitment of capital or the assumption of risk. It is open to discussion whether this approach is workable. Notably, in the context of Article 25 of the ICSID Convention (see section II.3 below), arbitral tribunals have treated characteristics of investments as cumulative, i.e. the investment exists only of all of the factors are present. Examples of a cumulative formulation can also be found in some treaties such as the Belgium/Luxembourg-Colombia BIT (2009) (Article I(2.3)).

(v) Time of establishing an investment

A further factor used in IIAs to delimit the scope of "investment" is a limitation based on the time of establishment. The agreement may exclude investment established prior to a certain date, such as the date on which an agreement is signed or enters into force. For example, Article 13 of the Egypt–Russian Federation BIT (1997) provides that "[t]*he present Agreement shall be applied with respect to all capital investments carried out by the investors of one of the Contracting Parties on the territory of the other Contracting Party, beginning in January 1 1987*". Developing countries sometimes seek to exclude investment established prior to entry into force of an investment protection agreement. For example Article 12 of the Cyprus-Egypt BIT (1998) states:

"*This Agreement shall apply to all investments made by investors of either Contracting Party in the territory of the other Contracting Party after its entry into force.*"

This excludes the possibility of an arbitral tribunal extending its jurisdiction to disputes that arise out of investments established before the agreement enters into force.

Most bilateral investment agreements do not specifically exclude pre-existing investment. Some of them even state explicitly that they do apply to existing investment. For example, Article 6 of the Estonia-Switzerland BIT (1992) provides that "[t]*he present Agreement shall also apply to investments in the territory of a Contracting Party made in accordance with its laws and regulations by investors of the other Contracting Party prior to the entry into force of this Agreement*". A similar provision can be found in the Austria-Philippines BIT (2002). The effect of such a provision is to ensure that an investment tribunal will have jurisdiction to hear any claim arising after the entry into force of the agreement but arising out of an investment made before the agreement entered force.

Few IIAs exclude investment established prior to some other date, such as the date on which the host country's foreign investment law entered into force. For example, Article 2 (3) of the Indonesia–United Kingdom BIT (1976) provides that "[t]*he rights and obligations of both Contracting Parties with respect to investments made before 10 January 1967 shall be in no way affected by the provisions of this Agreement*". This provision presumably was to exclude investment established prior to the entry into force of Indonesia's Foreign Capital Investment Law No. 1 of 1967. Indeed the Indonesian BITs with the United Kingdom (1977), Australia (1993) and Chile (1999) require that investments in Indonesia can only be protected if they are admitted in accordance with Law No 1 of 1967 and any law amending or replacing it.[28]

Some IIAs emphasize that prior investments are protected if approved by the host country's government. For example, Article 9 of the Egypt–Germany BIT (2005) provides that "[t]*he present Agreement shall also apply to investments by nationals or companies of either Contracting Party, made prior to the entering into force of this Agreement and accepted in accordance with the respective prevailing legislation of either Contracting Party*".

Timing of disputes. Some agreements that apply to investments made prior to as well as after the entry into force of the agreement may also deal with the timing of disputes. Thus, the agreement may specify that it applies only to disputes that arise after the entry into force of the agreement.[29] This requires the tribunal to determine when the dispute actually arises. For jurisdiction to be available, the dispute must arise after the treaty has entered into force. In this matter, the awards of tribunals do not offer a clear guide as there are inconsistent findings, though it is clear that the mere fact that the investment has ceased to exist by the time of the claim does not negate jurisdiction. Otherwise investments could be expropriated without any duty to pay compensation on the ground that there is no longer an owner of the investment (McLachlan et al. 2007, pp. 174–177).

(vi) Limiting to certain industry sectors

Other factors that could be used to limit the scope of the term "investment" are size and industry sector. Many countries, however, seek foreign investment from small and medium-sized companies and thus limitations on the size of investment are not common in investment agreements. The term "investment" may be limited to investment only in certain sectors of the economy. For example, Article 1 of the Energy Charter Treaty provides that "investment" refers to any investment associated with an Economic Activity in the Energy Sector and to investments or classes of investments designated by a Contracting Party in its Area as "Charter efficiency projects" and so notified to the Secretariat. In this particular case, the agreement was intended to cover only the energy sector and all its provisions were limited to that sector.

Another example can be found in the ASEAN Comprehensive Investment Agreement (2009), which applies, for the purposes of liberalization, to the following sectors: "*(a) manufacturing; (b) agriculture; (c) fishery; (d) forestry; (e) mining and quarrying; (f) services incidental to manufacturing, agriculture, fishery, forestry, mining and quarrying; and (g) any other sectors, as may be agreed upon by all Member States"* (Article 3(3)). Many IIAs exclude government procurement activities from their scope of application.

(vii) Intellectual property rights

As noted earlier, many agreements include intellectual property rights (IPRs) in the illustrative list of assets that are "investments". Such rights may include trademarks, trade secrets, patents and copyrights. In some investment agreements, the range of protected intellectual property includes also "technical processes" and "know-how", which are not legally protected as traditional forms of intellectual property. For example, the Romania–United Kingdom BIT (1999) follows this approach. This category also includes goodwill, an indication that the protected assets of a company may include not only its tangible property, but also its reputation. The transfer of intellectual property or know-how will count as a contribution to the development of the host country for purposes of being seen as an investment.[30]

Some BITs contain a very wide definition of IPRs which may raise significant concerns for the effectiveness of technology and skills transfer where host country policies may require this. For example the Japan–Peru BIT (2008) states in Article 1 (1) (f):

"(f) intellectual property rights, including copy rights and related rights, patent rights and rights relating to utility models, trademarks, industrial designs, layout-designs of integrated circuits, new varieties of plants, trade names, indications of source or geographical indications and undisclosed information; [...]

(h) any other tangible and intangible, movable and immovable property, and any related property rights, such as leases, mortgages, liens and pledges".[31]

This covers virtually any intangible right that the investor might enjoy. Given that tribunals are willing to accept IPRs and related rights to know-how, goodwill and other intangible rights as protected investments, this broad approach may have to be reconsidered where it might adversely affect the host country's right to regulate. Attention has to be given to ensuring consistence of the scope of protection offered by the IIA and domestic laws and regulations on IPRs.

4. The impact of article 25(1) of the ICSID Convention

A significant portion of IIA claims is adjudicated by arbitral tribunals convened under the ICSID Convention, which sets forth its own jurisdictional requirements. Article 25(1) of the Convention limits jurisdiction of arbitral tribunals to legal disputes *"arising directly out of an investment"*. The Executive Directors of the World Bank deliberately avoided including a definition of "investment" in the terms of Article 25(1) of the ICSID Convention, in part because there was no possibility of the Members coming to an agreement on the precise meaning of the term (Schreuer et al. 2009, pp. 114–117). Equally, this approach was designed to enable the Convention to accommodate both traditional types of investment, in the form of capital contributions, and new types of investment, including service contracts and transfers of technology (Delaume 1983, pp. 795; 1982, pp. 800–808).

The broad, non-exhaustive, nature of the asset-based definition of investment in BITs in particular, coupled with the fact that under Article 25(1) of the ICSID Convention the term "investment" is not defined, has led to a widening of the types of transactions that tribunals have accepted as investments. This has led to a possible blurring of the distinction between investments and other types of commercial transactions which has significant implications for the range of possible disputes that could come before arbitral tribunals. What might have been seen as purely commercial transactions at the time the IIA was signed could now be viewed as investments.

According to Gaillard, there are two basic approaches to the interpretation to the term "investment" in Article 25(1) that can be seen in awards and in scholarly analysis (Gaillard 2009). The first is a liberal intuitive method, which concentrates on the features of the transaction before the tribunal on a case-by-case basis, and the second is a deductive method that requires objective criteria which go beyond the subjective consent of the parties to the dispute to treat the transaction as an investment. The former is more likely to lead to a finding of jurisdiction while the later is more restrictive.

(i) Seeking flexibility in the definition of an investment

A liberal approach to defining investments can give greater flexibility in the protection of investments as these acquire more sophisticated forms. In this regard, investments can be seen often as bundles of transactions, some of which may be pure commercial contracts, but which together form an investment process. It is not always easy to unbundle such processes and to highlight the contractual nature of the transaction from which the claim arises and to ignore the context in which it occurs. As the ICSID tribunal in *CSOB v. Slovakia* stated:

> "*A dispute that is brought before the Centre must be deemed to arise directly out of an investment even when it is based on a transaction which, standing alone, would not qualify as an investment under the Convention, provided that the particular transaction forms an integral part of an overall operation that qualifies as an investment.*"[32]

Accordingly, it would not be prudent to lose this element of flexibility for investor protection given the way in which TNCs and other foreign investors are developing their operational processes. However this flexibility may need to be limited if it is misused to obtain access to international investment arbitration as a means of resolving problems arising out of the transaction concerned. The clearest illustration of this trend has been in relation to the widening of investments to include various financial and contractual processes (box 4).

Box 4. Examples of the widening scope of the term "investment"

According to the arbitral tribunal in *Mytilineos Holdings SA v. The State Union of Serbia & Montenegro and Republic of Serbia*, UNCITRAL, Partial Award, 8 September 2006, para. 113, 115:

"Examples from early ICSID practice include the construction of a chemical plant on a turn-key basis coupled with a management contract providing technical assistance for the operation of the plant as in Klöckner Industrie Anlagen GmbH v. Cameroon and Société Camerounaise des Engrais (SOCAME), Case ARB/81/2, a management contract for the operation of a cotton mill as in SEDITEX v. Madagascar, Case CONC/82/1, a contract for the conversion of vessels into fishing vessels and the training of crews as in Atlantic Triton Company Ltd v. Guinea, Case ARB/84/1, or technical and licensing agreements for the manufacturing of weapons as in Colt Industries Operating Corp, Firearms Div v. Republic of Korea, Case ARB/84/2. More recently financial instruments (Fedax N.V. v. Venezuela, ICSID Case No. ARB/96/3, Ceskoslovenska Obchodni Banka, a.s. v. The Slovak Republic, ICSID Case No. ARB/97/4), road constructions (Salini Costruttori S.p.A. and Italstrade S.p.A. v. Jordan, ICSID Case No. ARB/02/13; Salini Construtorri S.p.A. and Italstrade S.p.A. v. Morocco, ICSID Case No. ARB/00/4) and pre-shipment inspection arrangements

/...

Box 4 (concluded)

(SGS Société Générale de Surveillance S.A. v. Islamic Republic of Pakistan, ICSID Case No. ARB/01/13; SGS Société Générale de Surveillance S.A. v.Republic of the Philippines, ICSID Case No. ARB/02/6) have been regarded as investments under Article 25 of the ICSID Convention."

That said, arbitral awards interpreting BITs have distinguished between contractual arrangements that are investments and those that are not. Thus, contingent liabilities, such as bank guarantees, will not be regarded as "investments".[33] Nor will mere sales transactions unless expressly included in the definition of investment.[34] Pre-investment ·expenditure has been held not to constitute an "investment", though each such case will depend on its particular facts and, in particular, on the question whether the parties have agreed that such expenditure should be recoverable in the case of non-completion of the investment.[35] In addition, an investment contract may be held to exist even if certain terms remain to be agreed at a later date and where there is a possibility of renegotiation (Muchlinski 2007, pp. 732–733).[36]

(ii) The issue of objective requirements in the definition of "investment"

It was mentioned earlier that the arbitral interpretation of the broad asset-based definition of investment involves a determination of the interrelationship between the definition of "investment" in the BIT governing the particular transaction and the jurisdictional requirements of Article 25 (1) of the ICSID Convention. This has prompted tribunals to consider whether there are any mandatory definitional requirements stemming from the concept of "investment" that should control investor's rights to bring a claim before an ICSID tribunal. This is an issue specific to cases in which

ICSID arbitration is used, but one which has affected the analysis of the term even in ad hoc arbitrations governed by rules other than those of ICSID.[37]

(a) The ICSID Convention

Before the relevant awards are discussed, it is necessary first to examine the ICSID Convention itself. The Executive Directors of the World Bank deliberately avoided including a definition of "investment" in the terms of Article 25(1) of the ICSID Convention, in part because there was no possibility of the Members coming to an agreement on the precise meaning of the term (Schreuer et al. 2009, pp. 114–117). Equally, this approach was designed to enable the Convention to accommodate both traditional types of investment, in the form of capital contributions, and new types of investment, including service contracts and transfers of technology (Delaume 1983, pp. 795; 1982, pp. 800–808). The Executive Directors believed that adherence to the Convention by a country would provide an additional inducement for, and stimulate a larger flow of, private international investment into its territory. This was, in their opinion, the primary purpose of the Convention (IBRD 1965, p. 525, paras. 11-12). Thus, the ICSID Convention should not be seen merely as a means of dispute settlement. It is also *"an instrument of international policy for the promotion of economic development"* (Delaume 1986, p. 23; Schreuer et al. 2009, pp. 4-5). Indeed, the Preamble to the ICSID Convention speaks of, *"the need for international cooperation for economic development, and the role of private international investment therein."*

The precise meaning of this preambular statement lies at the heart of the differences in the various ICSID awards that have discussed the meaning of "investment". On the one hand, it has led some tribunals to declare that Article 25(1) introduces certain objective requirements, based on the nature and purpose of the ICSID Convention, which have to be present for a transaction to come within the meaning of "investment". Such an approach is justified by the view that ICSID jurisdiction cannot be left simply to the will of the parties to the IIA that offers the option of ICSID arbitration. Indeed, according to this line of awards, Article 25(1) will control the BIT, under which the claim is brought, so far as subject matter jurisdiction is concerned. Other tribunals have rejected this approach arguing that ICSID jurisdiction is not based on any pre-determined criteria but is founded on the applicable BIT.

(b) Awards favouring objective requirements

The leading example of the "objective requirements" approach is the case of *Salini v. Morocco*, where the Preambular reference to economic development was seen as an important factor in defining the nature of an investment for the purposes of ICSID jurisdiction (box 5). The case in effect establishes four requirements for there to be an investment over which an ICSID tribunal has jurisdiction. This case has been followed by other awards. Thus, in *Joy Mining v. Egypt*, a case arising out of a dispute over whether the claimant was entitled to the release of a bank guarantee, the tribunal states that for an arrangement to qualify as an "investment" it should have, *"a certain duration, a regularity of profit and return, an element of risk, a substantial commitment and that it should constitute a significant contribution to the host State's development"*.[38] In general, the development element should be met in most cases where the other elements, noted above, are shown to exist (Dolzer and Schreuer 2008, p. 69). The issue of a contribution to development was considered in the case of *Patrick Mitchell v. Congo* (see box 6).

Box 5. The case of *Salini Costruttori SpA and Italstrade Spa v. Kingdom of Morocco*

This case arose out of a non-payment by the respondent State to the claimants, two Italian construction companies, due to the late completion (by four months over the stipulated contractual completion period) of a highway construction contract entered into by the claimants with the Moroccan state highways company Société Nationale des Autoroutes du Maroc (ADM). The latter claimed that the project had been completed late in breach of contract, while the claimant maintained that the delay was due to external causes and not its failure to comply with the contract. On the issue of the definition of "investment" the tribunal stated:

"51. No definition of investment is given by the Convention. The two Parties recalled that such a definition had seemed unnecessary to the representatives of the States that negotiated it. Indeed, as indicated in the Report of the Executive Directors on the Convention: No attempt was made to define the term 'investment' given the essential requirement of consent by the parties, and the mechanism through which Contracting States can make known in advance, if they so desire, the classes of disputes which they would or would not consider submitting to the Centre (art. 25(4)).

52. The Tribunal notes that there have been almost no cases where the notion of investment within the meaning of Article 25 of the Convention was raised. However, it would be inaccurate to consider that the requirement that a dispute be 'in direct relation to an investment' is diluted by the consent of the Contracting Parties. To the contrary, ICSID case law and legal authors agree that the investment requirement must be respected as an objective condition of the jurisdiction of the Centre (cf. in particular, the commentary by E. Gaillard, in JDI 1999, p. 278 et seq., who cites the award rendered in 1975 in the Alcoa Minerals vs. Jamaica case as well as several other authors).

/...

Box 5 (continued)

The criteria to be used for the definition of an investment pursuant to the Convention would be easier to define if there were awards denying the Centre's jurisdiction on the basis of the transaction giving rise to the dispute. With the exception of a decision of the Secretary-General of ICSID refusing to register a request for arbitration dealing with a dispute arising out of a simple sale (I.F.I. Shihata and A.R. Parra, The Experience of the International Centre for Settlement of Investment Disputes: ICSID Review, Foreign Investment Law Journal, vol. 14, no. 2, 1999, p. 308)., the awards at hand only very rarely turned on the notion of investment. Notably, the first decision only came in 1997 (Fedax case, cited above). The criteria for characterization are, therefore, derived from cases in which the transaction giving rise to the dispute was considered to be an investment without there ever being a real discussion of the issue in almost all the cases.

The doctrine generally considers that investment infers: contributions, a certain duration of performance of the contact and a participation in the risks of the transaction (cf. commentary by E. Gaillard, cited above, p. 292). In reading the Convention's preamble, one may add the contribution to the economic development of the host State of the investment as an additional condition.

In reality, these various elements may be interdependent. Thus, the risks of the transaction may depend on the contributions and the duration of performance of the contract. As a result, these various criteria should be assessed globally even if, for the sake of reasoning, the Tribunal considers them individually here."

Source: Salini Costruttori SpA and Italstrade Spa v. Kingdom of Morocco, ICSID Case No. ARB/00/4, Decision on Jurisdiction, 23 July 2001 (42 *International Legal Materials* 609 (2003)).

Box 6. The Case of *Patrick Mitchell v. Democratic Republic of Congo*

In this case, a claim made by a United States lawyer working in his law firm in the Democratic Republic of the Congo, which he alleged was expropriated by the Democratic Republic of the Congo authorities by way of the firm's closure and the imprisonment of two of its lawyers, was rejected by the Annulment Committee on the grounds that the original tribunal had committed a manifest excess of powers and a failure to state reasons when they found that the legal practice was an investment under Article 25(1) of the ICSID Convention:

"28. The Preamble of the Washington Convention sets forth a number of basic principles as to its purpose and aims, which imbue the individual provisions of the Convention, including Article 25, which makes it needless to mention that the Convention was concluded under the auspices of the International Bank for Reconstruction and Development itself: 'Considering the need for international cooperation for economic development, and the role of private international investment therein;' […].

29. It is thus quite natural that the parameter of contributing to the economic development of the host State has always been taken into account, explicitly or implicitly, by ICSID arbitral tribunals in the context of their reasoning in applying the Convention, and quite independently from any provisions of agreements between parties or the relevant bilateral treaty.

30. Indeed, in the Salini case, the contribution to the economic development of the host State was explicitly set as a 'criterion' for an investment which was subsequently taken into account in respect of the construction of a highway, which led to the conclusion that

/...

Box 6 (continued)

the highway was clearly of public interest. Similarly, in the Fedax case, which involved promissory notes issued by the Republic of Venezuela to guarantee a loan equivalent to their amount, the arbitral tribunal observed that: "It is quite apparent that the transactions involved in this case are not ordinary commercial transactions and indeed involve a fundamental public interest [...] There is clearly a significant relationship between the transaction and the development of the host State." Finally, in the CSOB case, which involved a 'consolidation agreement' between the Czech Republic, Slovakia, and the Czechoslovak bank CSOB, with each of the two new States guaranteeing the reimbursement of the loan granted by CSOB to its national Collection Company, the Arbitral Tribunal observed that: "Under certain circumstances a loan may contribute substantially to a State's economic development [...] [The] undertaking involved a significant contribution by CSOB to the economic development of the Slovak Republic within the meaning of the Convention." While it is true that in these cases, where explicit reference was made to the "contribution to the economic development of the host State," the concept of investment was somewhat 'broadened,' this does nothing to alter the fundamental nature of that characteristic. It is thus found that, in another group of cases where the contribution to the economic development of the host State had not been mentioned expressly, it was doubtless covered by the very purpose of the contracts in question – all of which were State contracts – which had an obvious and unquestioned impact on the development of the host State.

31. In addition to the foregoing, it bears noting that Professor Schreuer regards the contribution to the economic development of the host State as 'the only possible indication of an objective

/...

Box 6 (continued)

meaning" of the term "investment.' In other words, the parties to an agreement and the States which conclude an investment treaty cannot open the jurisdiction of the Centre to any operation they might arbitrarily qualify as an investment. It is thus repeated that, before ICSID arbitral tribunals, the Washington Convention has supremacy over an agreement between the parties or a BIT.

32. This said, the problem does not arise in the case at hand, since not only are the aforementioned provisions of the Bilateral Treaty between the Democratic Republic of Congo and the United States altogether usual and in no way exorbitant, but the same Treaty also recognizes clearly in its Preamble that agreement upon the treatment to be accorded such investment will stimulate the flow of private capital and the economic development of both Parties. Moreover, this is a provision that appears in all bilateral treaties signed by the United States, and was even emphasized in the Preamble to the 2004 Model BIT.

33. The ad hoc Committee wishes nevertheless to specify that, in its view, the existence of a contribution to the economic development of the host State as an essential – although not sufficient – characteristic or unquestionable criterion of the investment, does not mean that this contribution must always be sizable or successful; and, of course, ICSID tribunals do not have to evaluate the real contribution of the operation in question. It suffices for the operation to contribute in one way or another to the economic development of the host State, and this concept of economic development is, in any event, extremely broad but also variable depending on the case."

Source: *Patrick Mitchell v. Democratic Republic of Congo*, ICSID Case No.ARB/99/7, Decision on Annulment, 1 November 2006.

The most extensive list of factors is found in the case *of Phoenix Action v. Czech Republic*:

"114. To summarize all the requirements for an investment to benefit from the international protection of ICSID, the Tribunal considers that the following six elements have to be taken into account:

1 – a contribution in money or other assets;

2 – a certain duration;

3 – an element of risk;

4 – an operation made in order to develop an economic activity in the host State;

5 – assets invested in accordance with the laws of the host State;

6 – assets invested bona fide.

115. The Tribunal wants to emphasize that an extensive scrutiny of all these requirements is not always necessary, as they are most often fulfilled on their face, "overlapping" or implicitly contained in others, and that they have to be analyzed with due consideration of all circumstances."[39]

In that case, the claimant alleged a number of breaches of the Czech Republic–Israel BIT (1997). According to the Czech Republic, Phoenix's claims fell outside the jurisdiction of the tribunal because Phoenix was, *"nothing more than an ex post facto creation of a sham Israeli entity created by a Czech fugitive from justice, Vladimír Beňo, to create diversity of nationality"*.[40] On the facts, the tribunal upheld this view, finding that the only purpose behind the creation of the claimant company was to gain access to ICSID procedures and not to make a *bona fide* investment.

Accordingly, the transactions in the case fell outside the ICSID definition of an "investment" and amounted to no more than an abuse of process.[41]

In a recent development, an ICSID tribunal dismissed – on an expedited basis as "manifestly without legal merit" – a claim that it considered to arise out of a purchase and sales contract and not out of an investment under the ICSID Convention.[42] The impact of this approach to defining "investment" has also been felt in cases brought outside ICSID. For example, in *Romak SA v. Uzbekistan*, a tribunal constituted under UNCITRAL Arbitration Rules adopted the following definition of "investment":

> *"The Arbitral Tribunal therefore considers that the term "investments" under the BIT has an inherent meaning (irrespective of whether the investor resorts to ICSID or UNCITRAL arbitral proceedings) entailing a <u>contribution</u> that extends over a <u>certain period of time</u> and that involves some <u>risk</u>."*[43]

The tribunal felt that whether there was an investment should be answered on the basis of the *"entire economic transaction that is the subject of these arbitral proceedings".*[44] The question at issue was whether a transfer of title to wheat from the claimant to the respondent amounted to an investment. Applying the above definition, the tribunal concluded that the claimant's interests did not constitute an investment because the transfer of title to wheat was a sales transaction and did not constitute a contribution in kind in furtherance of a venture, it did not reflect a commitment beyond a one-off transaction,[45] and did not involve risk typically associated with investment.[46] On this issue the tribunal stated:

> *"An 'investment risk' entails a different kind of alea, a situation in which the investor cannot be sure of a return on his investment, and may not know the amount he will end up spending, even if all relevant counterparties discharge their*

contractual obligations. Where there is "risk" of this sort, the investor simply cannot predict the outcome of the transaction".[47]

(c) Awards rejecting objective requirements

Other awards have refused to follow this deductive approach and have declared that there are no mandatory elements in the definition of investment under Article 25 (1). For example, in *Biwater v. Tanzania*, an ICSID claim brought by an operator of a water and sewerage services agreement after the respondent State purported to terminate the agreement, the tribunal held that there was little reason to use Article 25 (1) as a means of narrowing down the scope of the term "investment" as defined in the applicable BIT:

> *"Further, the Salini Test itself is problematic if, as some tribunals have found, the 'typical characteristics' of an investment as identified in that decision are elevated into a fixed and inflexible test, and if transactions are to be presumed excluded from the ICSID Convention unless each of the five criteria are satisfied. This risks the arbitrary exclusion of certain types of transaction from the scope of the Convention. It also leads to a definition that may contradict individual agreements (as here), as well as a developing consensus in parts of the world as to the meaning of 'investment' (as expressed, e.g., in bilateral investment treaties). If very substantial numbers of BITs across the world express the definition of 'investment' more broadly than the Salini Test, and if this constitutes any type of international consensus, it is difficult to see why the ICSID Convention ought to be read more narrowly."*[48]

In addition, the contribution to development requirement may be open to criticism as it introduces an element of motivation into the definition. This may not be relevant if the given definition of "investment" in the BIT is asset-based.[49] Indeed, it has been doubted whether the Preamble to the Convention can be read as implying a significant contribution to economic development as a condition of subject-matter jurisdiction. Thus in *Pey Casado v. Chile* the tribunal stated that:

> *"232. The present tribunal considers that there is a definition of investment under the ICSID Convention and that it is not enough to note the existence of certain 'characteristics' of an investment to determine whether the objective condition for the Center's jurisdiction is satisfied. Such an interpretation would render meaningless certain provisions of Article 25 of the ICSID Convention, which is not compatible with the requirement to interpret the terms of the Convention by giving them practical effect, as was rightly recalled by the decision in the case Joy Mining Machinery Limited v. Arab Republic of Egypt August 6, 2004.*
>
> *According to the tribunal, this definition comprises only three elements. The requirement of a contribution to the economic development of the host State, which is difficult to measure, seems to be a central element in the disputes, and not of the competence of the tribunal. It is true that the preamble of the ICSID convention mentions the contribution to economic development of host States. This reference is however presented as a consequence, and not as a condition of the investment: by protecting investments, the convention favors the development of host States. This does not mean that the economic development of the host State is encompassed in the notion of investment. This is the reason why this fourth condition is in fact included in the previous three conditions."*[unofficial translation][50]

Thus, the tribunal comes out clearly against the reading of a "contribution to development" as an essential component of an investment.

More recently, the validity of introducing the development criterion as a jurisdictional requirement has been criticized by the Annulment Committee in the case of *Malaysian Historical Salvors v. Malaysia*.[51] The question at issue was whether the salvage contract between the Government of Malaysia and Malaysian Historical Salvors was an "investment" for the purposes of Article 25(1) of the ICSID Convention. The original sole arbitrator held that it was not on the ground that, "*while the Contract did provide some benefit to Malaysia*", there was not "*a sufficient contribution to Malaysia's economic development to qualify as an 'investment' for the purposes of Article 25(1) or Article 1(a) of the BIT*".[52] The Annulment Committee disagreed. It felt that the arbitrator had failed to take into account the fact that Article 1 of the Malaysia–United Kingdom BIT (1981), under which the claimant brought his claim, contained a broad asset-based definition of investment whose purpose was to give a wide range of investments protection under the BIT.[53] Instead, the sole arbitrator used the approach taken in earlier awards to the interpretation of "investment" under Article 25 (1) of the ICSID Convention as the basis for interpreting the same term in the BIT as well.

According to the Annulment Committee, the contract was an investment as it was "one of a kind of asset" and in accordance with the definition in Article 1 of the BIT there was, "*a claim to money and to performance under a contract having financial value*". Furthermore, "*the contract involves intellectual property rights; and the right granted to salvage may be treated as a business concession conferred under contract*".[54] The Annulment Committee went on to criticize the decision of the sole arbitrator on the grounds that:

> "*(a) it altogether failed to take account of and apply the Agreement between Malaysia and the United Kingdom defining "investment" in broad and encompassing terms but rather limited itself to its analysis of criteria which it found to bear*

upon the interpretation of Article 25(1) of the ICSID Convention;

(b) its analysis of these criteria elevated them to jurisdictional conditions, and exigently interpreted the alleged condition of a contribution to the economic development of the host State so as to exclude small contributions, and contributions of a cultural and historical nature;

(c) it failed to take account of the preparatory work of the ICSID Convention and, in particular, reached conclusions not consonant with the travaux in key respects, notably the decisions of the drafters of the ICSID Convention to reject a monetary floor in the amount of an investment, to reject specification of its duration, to leave 'investment' undefined, and to accord great weight to the definition of investment agreed by the Parties in the instrument providing for recourse to ICSID."[55]

Accordingly, the majority of the annulment committee concluded that the sole arbitrator had manifestly exceeded his powers in making this decision.

The majority decision was strongly criticized by Judge Mohamed Shahabuddeen in his dissenting opinion. He felt that the ICSID Convention set certain "outer limits" to the meaning of an "investment" based on the fact that a major aim of the Convention was to encourage the economic development of member countries by way of investment. Thus, it was perfectly reasonable to read that term as requiring a contribution to the economic development of the host country. Judge Shahabuddeen stated:

"In this connection, it is possible to conceive of an entity which is systematically earning its wealth at the expense of the development of the host State. However, much that may collide with a prospect of development of the host State, it would not breach a condition – on the argument of the Applicant.

Accordingly, such an entity would be entitled to claim the protection of ICSID. Host States which let in purely commercial enterprises would have something to worry about. Correspondingly, ICSID would seem to have lost its way: it is time to call back the organization to its original mission."[56]

That original mission was, in the judge's view, to provide a dispute settlement mechanism for investments that made a positive contribution to the economic development of the host country. According to him, it was Article 25(1) that governed the definition of investments for the purposes of taking the dispute to ICSID, not the terms of the BIT. Otherwise the parties could determine the jurisdiction of ICSID and Article 25(1) would be rendered meaningless.[57]

The disagreement between the majority of the annulment committee and Judge Shahabuddeen encapsulates the dilemma in international investment law as to whether it is a law of investment protection, pure and simple, in which case the notion of investment must be given as wide a compass as possible so that access to dispute settlement procedures is made easier for the investor, or whether it is a law of international economic cooperation, in which case the need for a balancing of the private interests of the investor and the public interests of the host country may be essential. On this approach, the requirement of a significant contribution to development arising out of the investment may be seen as a key jurisdictional prerequisite. It remains to be seen whether ICSID tribunals will follow the majority position in Malaysian Salvors and ignore the development criterion or continue to apply it. The development implications of this approach will be discussed in Section III.

5. "Investment" and group structures in TNCs

(i) Indirect investment and issues of ownership and control

The broad asset-based definition includes, as noted above, various types of interests in companies including stockholding that can be held directly or indirectly. This has significant implications for the way in which the term "investment" may be seen when applied to the situation of complex transnational corporate groups. Such groups operate a network of owned and controlled holding and subsidiary companies that together form an integrated enterprise across national borders. Given the breadth of the term "interests in companies" this raises the possibility that an "investment" by a TNC could comprise not only of the locally incorporated subsidiary, by reason of its foreign controlling ownership, but also the intermediate holding company as the direct owner of the subsidiary. In the case of groups of companies it means in effect that a corporate entity in the host country can be an "investor" and can also be part of the enterprise that constitutes the "investment" (figure 3).

Furthermore, the natural persons who hold shares in any of these companies might also have a claim based on their investment in the group as outside shareholders. The analysis of whether such investments come within the IIA is closely tied up to the definition of "investor" as well, and will be discussed below (see Section II.B).

The existence of complex group structures may require the IIA to clarify issues of ownership and control. Some agreements include a definition of these terms for the purposes of determining the existence of an investment. For example, the Japan–Peru BIT (2008) states in Article 1 (3):

"An enterprise is:

(a) 'owned' by an investor if more than 50 percent of the equity interest in it is owned by the investor;

(b) *'controlled' by an investor if the investor has the power to name a majority of its directors or otherwise to legally direct its actions; and*

(c) *'affiliated' with an investor when it controls, or is controlled by, the investor; or when it and the investor are both controlled by the same investor."*

Figure 3. Example of an indirect investment (group structure)

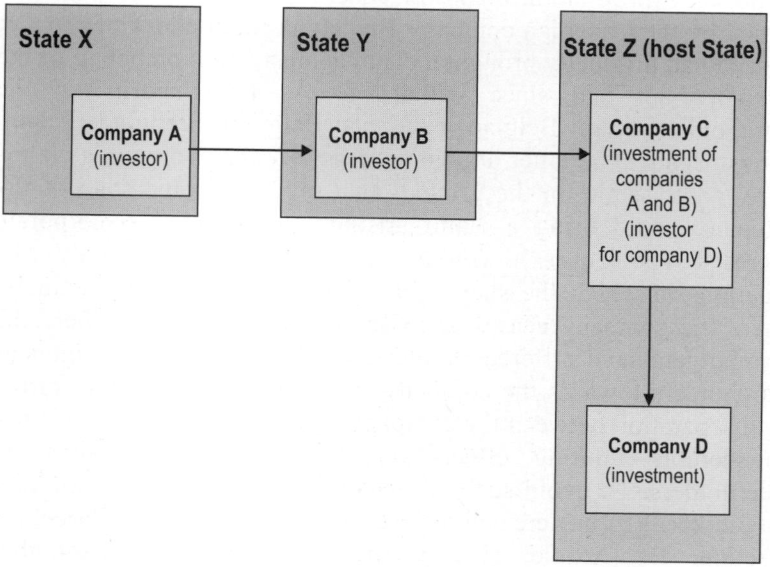

(ii) The impact of public international law rules on corporate nationality

A further problem concerns the relationship between the general international law rules on corporate nationality and their applicability to investment law. Under public international law, in the light of the *Barcelona Traction Case* (ICJ 1970) and, more recently, the *Diallo Case* (ICJ 2007), a narrow approach to corporate nationality has prevailed and the right of diplomatic protection has been limited to the state of incorporation or of the seat of the company. The *Barcelona Traction Case* arose out of the purported expropriation of power generating facilities in Catalonia owned by the Canadian company Barcelona Light and Traction Co. Canada had originally brought a claim against Spain on behalf of the company but had since withdrawn. As the majority of the shareholders were Belgian nationals Belgium brought a claim against Spain. The latter argued successfully that Belgium's claims were inadmissible on the grounds that only the home state of the company could bring a claim arising out of harm to corporate interests. The Court in *Barcelona Traction* admitted only two situations in which the shareholder's State can intervene, namely, where the company ceases to exist as a legal entity or where the shareholders have suffered an interference with their direct rights as shareholders towards the company. The Court relied on the formal legal separation between the company and its shareholders. This has considerable limiting effects on the bringing of claims by shareholders. To avoid such an outcome the ICSID Convention by Article 25(2)(b) has created an exception to the logic of Barcelona Traction. By Article 25(2)(b) the term "national of another Contracting State" includes, for the purposes of Article 25(1):

"[...] *any juridical person which had the nationality of a Contracting State other than the State party to the dispute on the date on which the parties consented to submit such dispute to conciliation or arbitration* **and any juridical person which had the nationality of the Contracting State party to the** *dispute on that date and which, because of foreign control, the parties have agreed should be treated as a national of another contracting state for the purposes of this Convention".* (Emphasis added)

The second part of the sentence ensures that claims made by direct controlling foreign shareholders in a locally incorporated subsidiary can bring claims before ICSID. This is significant from a definitional perspective as it makes clear that formal legal separation between a local subsidiary and its foreign controlling interest will not deny the foreign character to the subsidiary, thereby allowing claims to be made by the local subsidiary itself.

A number of IIAs employ another way to deal with the same issue: they entitle a foreign investor to bring claims not only on its own behalf but also on behalf of the host-State enterprise which it owns or controls (this is typical for IIAs that use the enterprise-based definition of investment) (see Section II.A.(1)). For instance, Article 11(2) of the Mexico–Singapore BIT (2009) entitles an investor to bring a claim *"on behalf of an enterprise legally constituted pursuant to the laws of the other Contracting Party that is a legal person such investor owns or controls, directly or indirectly"*. This provides an opportunity for the investor to recover the damage suffered by the enterprise, which can be different from the damage suffered by the investor as a shareholder. Moreover, where the investor does not have full ownership, this approach should make it possible to recover all damages of the enterprise and not only the part proportionate to the shareholder's stake in the company.

(iii) Claims of parent and holding companies and minority shareholders

Claims made by parent and holding companies arising out of their direct investments in subsidiaries are not uncommon. They are seen by tribunals as within the jurisdiction of BITs containing references to interests in companies as a category of protected investment (Dolzer and Schreuer 2008, pp. 54–55). It is this fact that has led to the use of holding or shell companies, incorporated in jurisdictions enjoying investment treaty relations with host countries, as a means of enhancing protection under IIAs, especially where the home country of the parent company has no treaty in place with a given host country. The implications of this situation will be further considered below.

Unlike the requirements of Article 25(2)(b) of the ICSID Convention, the reference to interests in companies in BITs does not require that the investor's interest or participation in the company be a controlling one. Indeed, minority shareholdings are generally protected under IIAs and arbitral tribunals have supported this approach (McLachlan et al. 2007, pp. 187–189). For example, in the case of *CMS Gas Transmission Co v. Argentina* the tribunal states:

"Precisely because the [ICSID] Convention does not define 'investment', it does not purport to define the requirements that an investment should meet to qualify for ICSID jurisdiction. There is indeed no requirement that an investment, in order to qualify, must necessarily be made by shareholders controlling a company or owning the majority of its shares. It is well known incidentally that, depending on how shares are distributed, controlling shareholders can in fact own less than the majority of shares. The reference that Article 25 (2) (b) makes to foreign control in terms of treating a company of the nationality of the Contracting State party as a national of another Contracting State is precisely meant to facilitate agreement between the parties, so as not to have the corporate personality interfering with the protection of the real interests associated with the investment. The same result can be achieved by means of the provisions of the BIT, where the consent may include non-controlling or minority shareholders."[58]

This statement has been cited with approval in many other cases and represents a settled approach of arbitral tribunals (McLachlan et al. 2007, p. 188 and cases cited therein).

(iv)The risk of multiple claims

The impact for a State of such an approach to complex group structures will be felt mainly in relation to the risk of multiple claims being made on the basis of the same investment by various classes of shareholders. This could expose the host country to considerable legal pressure and uncertainty, as well as risk the creation of inconsistent decisions by domestic and/or various international tribunals involving different claimants from the TNC group and its outside shareholders. Such events may contribute to the lack of predictability in the investment arbitration process.

The potential for multiple claims is well illustrated by the case brought by the American entrepreneur Ronald Lauder against the Czech Republic arising out of the dispute over the Czech TV station TV Nova. Mr. Lauder had set up this station but lost control over it in circumstances which he alleged had been engineered by the Czech State amounting to a breach of his rights against expropriation under the Czech Republic-United States BIT (1991) in relation to his own losses as the ultimate owner, and under the Czech Republic-Netherlands BIT (1991) in relation to the losses alleged to have been suffered by the Netherlands holding company of TV Nova. The first case *Lauder v. Czech Republic*[59] was unsuccessful. On the other hand, the claim brought by the holding company *CME Czech Republic v. Czech Republic*[60] was successful, even though the facts of each case were identical. Both tribunals noted that the Czech Republic had refused an offer of consolidation of the claims. Equally, both tribunals felt that they were entitled to act independently and to come to their own decisions as each tribunal was dealing with a different BIT and with different parties.

In addition, the CME tribunal held that this was not a proper case in which to apply a "single economic entity" or "company group" theory, which was generally not accepted in international arbitration especially as in this case Mr. Lauder was not the majority shareholder in CME even though he was the ultimate controller of the group.[61]

To avoid such an outcome, a host country may wish to ensure that a control-based test of corporate nationality is included in its IIAs so that the tribunal is enabled to lift the corporate veil and to see the true nationality of the ultimate controller. Alternatively, an (automatic) denial-of-benefits clause would deprive the intermediate holding company of the IIA protection, provided that it does not engage in substantial business operations in the State of incorporation (see section II.B.(2)(d)).

B. Investor

Investment agreements apply typically only to investment by investors who qualify for coverage. The definition of the term "investor" is thus as important in determining the scope of an agreement as that of "investment". The definition of "investor" normally includes natural persons and artificial or legal persons (or juridical entities). As noted earlier, with respect to natural persons, the main issue that arises is that of determining the relevant link between the investor and his/her home State party to an agreement. Legal entities, by contrast, can be defined to include or exclude a number of different types of entity. Generally speaking, legal entities may be excluded because of their legal form, their purpose or their ownership.

Arbitral tribunals have interpreted the definitions of "investor" and the concept of "nationality" in ways that have significant implications for the application of IIAs. Recent awards have concentrated on two particular issues. First, in order to determine jurisdiction, *ratione personae* arbitral tribunals have considered the relevant criteria for determining the nationality of natural and/or legal persons. Secondly, tribunals have considered what rights of standing minority shareholders, non-controlling and indirect shareholders may have under investor-state dispute settlement provisions of IIAs (UNCTAD 2007b, p. 9). This mirrors the question of whether such minority and indirect interests can be considered investments, which was discussed above (see Section II.A.5(a) and (c)).

1. Natural persons

(i) Nationality links

Natural persons are considered "investors" within the meaning of an agreement only if they have the nationality of a State party to an IIA or, in a number of cases, if they are linked to that State in another manner, such through permanent residence, domicile or residence. Under customary international law, a State may not be required to recognize the nationality of a person unless the person has a genuine link with the State of asserted nationality (*Nottebohm Case*).[62] Most investment agreements do not require such a link, at least in the case of natural persons. Indeed, by Article 25(2) of the ICSID Convention, a different criterion, the nationality at the date of consent to submission of a dispute to ICSID, is more important:

"'National of another Contracting State' means:

(a) any natural person who had the nationality of a Contracting State other than the State party to the dispute on the date on which the parties consented to submit such dispute to conciliation or arbitration as well as on the date on which the request was registered pursuant to paragraph (3) of Article 28 or paragraph (3) of Article 36, **but does not include any person**

who on either date also had the nationality of the Contracting State party to the dispute." (Emphasis added.)

The common practice in investment agreements (as in more general international practice) is that a natural person possesses the nationality of a State if the law of that State so provides. For example, Article 1(2)(b) of the Ethiopia–Spain BIT (2006) defines nationals as "*physical persons who, according to the law of that Contracting Party, are considered to be its nationals*". This language limits the nationality test to the formal requirement of citizenship and does not require that there be a genuine link between the person and the state of asserted nationality.

(ii) Other links

Certain investment agreements may, however, require some link beyond nationality. For example, the Germany–Israel BIT (1976) provides, in Article 1 (3) (b), that the term "nationals" means, with respect to Israel, "*Israeli nationals being permanent residents of the State of Israel*". Equally, the new ASEAN Comprehensive Investment Agreement (2009) goes beyond its predecessor (the ASEAN Agreement for Promotion and Protection of Investments of 1987) and defines "natural person" as "*any natural person possessing the nationality or citizenship of, **or right of permanent residence in the Member State** in accordance with its laws, regulations and national policies*" (emphasis added). On the other hand, a concept like permanent residence can be used not only in addition to a nationality link but also as an alternative. The latter may be especially in the interest of high immigration countries in which a considerable proportion of the economically active population may not yet be full citizens. Such countries (e.g. Australia, Canada and the United States) regularly extend a special legal status to permanent residents. For example, Article 1(c) of the Argentina–Australia BIT (1995) defines a natural person as an "investor" as follows:

"(i) in respect of Australia:
(A) a natural person who is a citizen or permanent resident of Australia; [...] and
(ii) in respect of the Argentine Republic:
(A) a natural person who is a national of the Argentine Republic in accordance with its laws on nationality [...]"

Here, a difference in approach is enshrined between Australian investors and Argentine investors. The former may not necessarily be a citizen as permanent residence suffices while the latter need only be a national under Argentine nationality laws.

Other IIAs allow a natural person to claim, for the purposes of the agreement, the nationality of a country or some other basis, such as residency or domicile in that country. For example, Article 3.1 of the Treaty Establishing the Caribbean Community (CARICOM) Agreement on the Harmonization of Fiscal Incentives to Industry defines "national" to mean *"a person who is a citizen of any Member State and includes a person who has a connection with such a State of a kind which entitles him to be regarded as belonging to or, if it be so expressed, as being a native or resident of the State for the purpose of such laws thereof relating to immigration as are for the time being, in force"*.

(iii) The problem of home and host country dual nationality

One question not explicitly addressed by most IIAs is whether a natural person is a covered investor if he or she possesses the nationality of both the home and the host countries which are parties to the agreement. This issue is likely to arise in particular in an investment agreement that provides for the protection of foreign investment. As noted earlier, under customary international law, a State could exercise diplomatic protection on behalf of one of its nationals with respect to a claim against another State, even if its national also possessed the nationality of the other State, provided that the dominant and effective nationality of the person was of the State exercising diplomatic protection (*Nottebohm Case* and *Barcelona Traction Case*).[63] This test, however, typically is not found in existing IIAs, which, as noted, tend to be silent on the matter of dual nationality. The effective link test has also been rejected by arbitral tribunals which have had to determine whether the claimant, a natural person, possesses the nationality of a Contracting Party other than the host Contracting Party country for the purposes of the ICSID Convention.[64] Most recently, in the case of *Micula v. Romania*, where the claimants' Swedish nationality was doubted by the Respondent State, Romania, on the grounds that they had no effective links with Sweden but only with Romania, the tribunal held that:

> "100. The Tribunal must [...] examine whether there is any room for the Nottebohm requirement of a 'genuine link' in this proceeding. There is little support for the proposition that the genuine link test has any role to play in the context of ICSID proceedings. The ICSID Convention requires only that a claimant demonstrate that it is a national of a 'Contracting State'. In fact, Article 25(2) (a) of the ICSID Convention does not require that a claimant hold solely one nationality, so long as its second nationality is not that of the State party to the dispute. The Tribunal agrees with the conclusion of the tribunal in Siag that the regime established under Article 25 of the ICSID Convention does not leave room for a test of dominant or effective nationality. No previous ICSID tribunal appears to have ever ruled to the contrary and Respondent has not supplied any convincing evidence to the contrary. In fact, Respondent has not convinced the Tribunal to hold otherwise."[65]

The tribunal went on to consider the effect of the Romania-Sweden BIT (2002), which applied to the case:

"101. It is also doubtful whether the genuine link test would apply pursuant to the BIT. The Contracting Parties to the BIT are free to agree whether any additional standards must be applied to the determination of nationality. Sweden and Romania agreed in the BIT that the Swedish nationality of an individual would be determined under Swedish law and included no additional requirements for the determination of Swedish nationality. The Tribunal concurs with the Siag tribunal that the clear definition and the specific regime established by the terms of the BIT should prevail and that to hold otherwise would result in an illegitimate revision of the BIT."

Given that the claimants' Swedish nationality was validly obtained under Swedish law, there was no doubt that they were nationals of another ICSID Contracting Party and of the other Contracting Party to the BIT.

Some treaties do have rules on how to deal with dual nationality where one nationality is that of a non-Contracting Party. Thus Article 1 of the United States-Uruguay (2005) treaty defines "investor of a Party" in the following way:

"Article 1
Definitions
*'investor of a Party' means a Party or State enterprise thereof, or a national or an enterprise of a Party, that attempts to make, is making, or has made an investment in the territory of the other Party; **provided, however, that a natural person who is a dual citizen shall be deemed to be exclusively a citizen of the State of his or her dominant and effective citizenship."***
(Emphasis added.)

Article 17.3 of the Convention Establishing the Inter-Arab Investment Guarantee Corporation has similar language, but states even more explicitly in Article 17.1 that:

"[i]*n no event shall the investor be **a natural person who is a national of the host country** or a juridical person whose main seat is located in such country if its stocks and shares are substantially owned by this country or its nationals.*" (Emphasis added.)

Another agreement addressing dual nationality is the Canada–Lebanon BIT (1997). It states:

"*Article 1*
Definitions
'investor' means:
*any natural person possessing the citizenship of or permanently residing in one Contracting Party in accordance with its laws; ... who makes the investment in the territory of the other Contracting Party. **In the case of persons who have both Canadian and Lebanese citizenship, they shall be considered Canadian citizens in Canada and Lebanese citizens in Lebanon.**"* (Emphasis added.)

The literal language of many agreements requires that the host country protect investment owned by nationals of the other party, and nothing explicitly states that this obligation lapses where the investors happen also to be nationals of the host country. A host country may argue that limitations on the rights of dual nationals are implied, but a country that does not wish to extend treaty coverage to investment owned by dual nationals would be well advised to insert explicit language to that effect in the agreement. This may be particularly important where the investor, a natural person, uses a legal entity established in the other Contracting Party to bring a claim. In such a case, the claimant may well be protected under the applicable IIA even if the natural person does not possess the nationality of one of the Contracting Parties. Such a possibility was held out to be a solution to the lack of Contracting Party nationality on the part of the claimant in the case of *Soufraki v. The United Arab Emirates*.[66] The claimant was a dual Italian and Canadian national but had allowed his Italian nationality to lapse. Thus, he could not bring a claim under the Italy–United Arab Emirates BIT. The tribunal held that, *"had Mr. Soufraki contracted with the United Arab Emirates through a corporate vehicle incorporated in Italy, rather than contracting in his personal capacity, no problem of jurisdiction would now arise"*.[67] This is another example of "treaty shopping" which is further discussed in Section 2.B.(2)(c).

(iv) Implications for treaty negotiation

The recent trend in arbitral interpretations of when natural persons qualify as investors on grounds of their nationality has important negotiating implications. First, not only the impact of the wording used in the BIT should be taken into account but also the impact of Article 25 of the ICSID Convention when it comes to determining nationality for the purposes of the ICSID Convention. Second, the central role of national legislation in determining nationality for these purposes may not always exclude problems of dual or uncertain nationality. Though tribunals will not in general second guess decisions of national authorities in these matters, they may not be able to ignore manifest errors either. Accordingly it may be prudent to include language dealing with problems of dual and/or uncertain nationality in the relevant IIA.

Some recent agreements have included a dominant of effective nationality test. For example, the Rwanda–United States BIT (2008) states:

"[...] 'investor of a Party' means a Party or State enterprise thereof, or a national or an enterprise of a Party, that attempts to make, is making, or has made an investment in the territory of

*the other Party; **provided, however, that a natural person who is a dual national shall be deemed to be exclusively a national of the State of his or her dominant and effective nationality.***"
(Emphasis added.)

Should that effective nationality come to be the same as that of the host respondent State in an ICSID claim, then Article 25 (2) would operate to exclude that claim. Equally, where the BIT allows permanent residents to be protected under its terms, this too might not be sufficient for ICSID jurisdiction to be allowed where the effective nationality is that of a State that is not a Party to the ICSID Convention (UNCTAD 2007b, p. 12).

2. Legal entities

(i) Range of entities covered

Legal entities can be defined to include or exclude a number of different types of entity. In this context, a State may wish to consider whether to include entities without legal personality, branches of enterprises, non-profit entities and government-owned entities. Some IIAs only cover those entities that have legal personality, while others also include those without it. For example, German BITs consistently mention entities "*with or without legal personality*" in order to protect those German undertakings that operate without adopting a separate legal personality. Some IIAs further specify that the term "investor" also includes branches of legal entities (see, for example, Canada-Jordan BIT (2009), Article 1(j) and 1(t)).

Treaty-makers can further consider whether or not to cover non-profit entities (educational, charitable or other). The Mexico-Singapore BIT (2009), as well as many others, explicitly covers non-profit organization (Article 1(2) and 1(8)). The kinds of activities in which a non-profit entity engages may produce desirable forms of investment, such as a research facility or a hospital. Further, non-profit entities often acquire shares in commercial enterprises in order to earn revenue to support their charitable or educational activities. In that capacity, non-profit entities are likely to act in the same way as any other portfolio investor and their distinct status as non-profit entities would seem of little significance.

Finally, States that actively pursue investment activities, either directly or through government–owned entities, including sovereign wealth funds, may wish to ensure that the relevant entities are covered. Many IIAs expressly mention government-owned entities. Perhaps the most vivid example can be found in the BIT concluded by Saudi Arabia that includes in the definition of investor "the Government of the Kingdom of Saudi Arabia and its financial institutions and authorities such as the Saudi Arabian Monetary Agency, public funds and other similar governmental institutions existing in Saudi Arabia" (Article 1(3) of the Malaysia–Saudi Arabia BIT (2000)).

(ii) Tests of corporate nationality

In the case of legal entities, most investment agreements use one of three different criteria for determining nationality: the country of organization or incorporation, the country of the seat or the country of ownership or control. In many cases, they use some combination of these criteria. Other criteria are occasionally used as well.

Country of organization/incorporation. An example of an agreement using the place of organization as the criterion of nationality is the Energy Charter Treaty, which in Article 1 (7) (a) (ii) defines "investor" with respect to a Contracting Party to include "*a company or other organization organized in accordance with the law applicable in that Contracting Party*". Similarly, the Rwanda–United States BIT (2008) states:

*"'enterprise' means any entity **constituted or organized under applicable law**, whether or not for profit, and whether privately or governmentally owned or controlled, including a corporation, trust, partnership, sole proprietorship, joint venture, association, or similar organization; **and a branch of an enterprise.***

'enterprise of a Party' **means an enterprise constituted or organized under the law of a Party, and a branch located in the territory of a Party and carrying out business activities there**" (Emphasis added).

The use of country-of-organization is consistent with the decision of the International Court of Justice in Barcelona Traction.[68]

The advantage of using the country-of-organization test is ease of application, as there usually will not be any doubt concerning the country under whose law a company is organized. Further, the country-of-organization is not easily changed, meaning that the nationality of the investor usually will be permanent under this approach. Because an important purpose of some investment agreements is to attract investment by providing a stable investment regime and because changes in the nationality of an investor will result in the loss of treaty protection for investment owned by the investor, a definition of "investor" that stabilizes the nationality of the investor and thus the protection afforded to investment is particularly consistent with the purposes of IIAs.

The disadvantage of using country-of-organization is that the link between the investor and its country of nationality may be insignificant. Under this test, a company may claim the nationality of a particular country even though no nationals of that country participate in the ownership or management of the company and even though the company engages in no activity in that country. In effect, the company could claim the benefits of nationality of a particular country, including protection under the treaties of that country, despite the fact that it conferred no economic benefit of any kind on that country. This should perhaps be of concern principally to the home country, which finds itself protecting an investor that brings it no economic benefit. It may also be of concern to the host country, however. The effect of this test may be that the host country is extending protection to investment ultimately owned by persons who live in a country that extends no reciprocal benefits to the host country's own investors. Indeed, the country of ownership or control may not even have normal economic relations with the host country. To address this potential problem, IIAs using the place of incorporation as the sole criterion to determine nationality of a legal entity often also include a denial-of-benefits clause (see Section 2.B.(2)(c)).

Country of company seat. Turning to the company seat approach, an example of a treaty using this test as the basis for attributing nationality is the 2005 German model BIT. That treaty defines "company" in Article 1(3) (a) to include in respect of Germany *"any juridical person as well as any commercial or other company or association with or without legal personality **having its seat in the territory of the Federal Republic of Germany"*** (emphasis added).[69] The seat of a company may not be as easy to determine as the country of organization, but it does reflect a more significant economic relationship between the company and the country of nationality. Generally speaking, "seat of a company" connotes the place where effective management takes place. The seat is also likely to be relatively permanent as well. To strengthen the country-of-seat test further and avoid granting protection to "mail-box" companies, some IIAs provide that to be eligible as an investor of a contracting party, a legal entity must carry out "real economic activities" (Colombia-Switzerland BIT (2006), Article 1(2)(b)) or engage in "business activities" (Canada-Jordan BIT (2009), Article 1(k)) in the territory of a that party.

Country of ownership or control. The country-of-ownership or control criterion means that a legal entity will be considered an investor of a State whose nationals own or control it. This test may be the most difficult to ascertain and the least permanent, particularly in the case of companies whose stock is traded on major stock exchanges. Its principal benefit as a test is that it links coverage by an agreement with a genuine economic link. Perhaps for these reasons, the ownership or control test sometimes is used in conjunction with one of the other tests. Combining the criteria in this way lends a degree of certainty and permanence to the test of nationality, while also ensuring that treaty coverage and economic benefit are linked. The control test is of great relevance when dealing with issues of multiple claims by discrete members of a corporate group and also as a means of controlling treaty shopping.

(iii) Problems arising out of formal country-of-organization test

(a) Standing of locally incorporated subsidiaries

A further problem already alluded to above is that the use of a country of organization test can lead to odd results in the context of a complex corporate group structure. As noted above, in accordance with the *Barcelona Traction Case*, given that the locally incorporated subsidiary of a foreign parent company has the corporate nationality of the host country, under customary international law the subsidiary cannot bring a claim against that country. In order to avoid this situation, the ICSID Convention allows for the use of a test of foreign control coupled with the consent of the host country to treat the local subsidiary as a foreign national for the purposes of ICSID jurisdiction. Thus by Article 25(2)(b) of the ICSID Convention the term "national of another contracting State" means, for the purposes of Article 25(1):

"any juridical person which had the nationality of a Contracting State other than the State party to the dispute on the date on

*which the parties consented to submit such dispute to conciliation or arbitration **and any juridical person which had the nationality of the Contracting State party to the dispute on that date and which, because of foreign control, the parties have agreed should be treated as a national of another contracting state for the purposes of this Convention.***" (Emphasis added)

The purpose of this part of Article 25(2)(b) is to ensure that foreign investments carried out by means of a locally incorporated subsidiary or joint venture are not excluded from the ICSID Convention. If that were so, then a major category of claims based on the treatment of local subsidiaries would fall outside the scope of the Convention, causing it to lose much of its utility. Thus the ICSID Convention goes beyond the limitations laid down in the *Barcelona Traction Case*, concerning the protection of foreign shareholders in a locally incorporated company (Muchlinski 2007, p. 727). The host Contracting Party is given discretion over whether to extend ICSID arbitration to locally incorporated entities. The extent of this discretion has been clarified in the decisions of ICSID tribunals (Asouzu 2002). On the issue of consent, tribunals have been ready to find this not only in cases of express consent but also in cases where this can be implied (Muchlinski 2007, pp. 727-728). Thus, if a host State wishes to restrict ICSID arbitration only to disputes between the parent company and itself, this should be made explicit.

As regards the criterion of foreign control, in *Vacuum Salt v. Ghana*[70] the tribunal held that agreement to treat a claimant as a foreign national does not ipso facto confer jurisdiction. The requirement of "foreign control" in Article 25(2)(b) sets an objective limit beyond which jurisdiction cannot be granted.[71] Accordingly a 20 per cent holding by a Greek national in Ghanaian incorporated Vacuum Salt was, in the circumstances, insufficient to show foreign control, given that he did not exercise anything other than a technical advisory function and that the remaining 80 per cent of the equity, and actual managerial control, was in Ghanaian hands.[72] In Vacuum Salt, the fact that the majority of the controlling interests possessed the nationality of the host country party to the dispute was sufficient to dispose of jurisdiction. In *Aguas del Tunari SA v. Bolivia*, the tribunal gave a detailed analysis of the meaning and application of the term "controlled directly or indirectly" in the Bolivia-Netherlands BIT (1992), where the question of actual control by Dutch nationals of the Bolivian claimant company was at issue for the purposes of jurisdiction. Bolivia claimed that the Dutch holding companies were mere shells and that the real nationality of control was that of the ultimate United States parent. The tribunal held that the Dutch companies were in actual control of the Bolivian claimant company and so it was an entity under control from the Netherlands for the purposes of the BIT.[73]

> (b) *Making investments through intermediate companies: The problem of "treaty shopping"*

In the more recent case of *Tokios Tokelés v. Ukraine* the factor of foreign control appears to have been diluted.[74] This and other cases reviewed below suggest that an investor from a third State, or even from the host State itself, can obtain the benefits of IIA protection by channelling its investment through an intermediate holding company incorporated in a State which has an IIA with the host State (see figures 4 and 5). The possibilities for such "treaty shopping" are created by permissive language of many IIAs, which define "investor" solely by reference to the country of incorporation.

In *Tokios Tokelés v. Ukraine*, the majority of the tribunal held that a company incorporated in Lithuania, but owned and controlled by Ukrainian nationals (who owned 99 per cent of the shares and formed two thirds of the management), was a Lithuanian national for the purposes of Article 25(2)(b). As this provision was aimed at expanding, and not restricting, the jurisdiction of ICSID so long as the formal nationality of incorporation was that of another Contracting Party the tribunal would not "lift the corporate veil".[75] This conclusion was reinforced by the fact that the BIT defined an "investor" of Lithuania under Article 1(2)(b) as an "entity established in the territory of the Republic of Lithuania in conformity with its laws and regulations." This method of defining corporate nationality was found by the tribunal to be consistent with modern BIT practice and that it satisfied the requirements of Article 25.[76] In addition, the company had been incorporated six years before the Lithuania–Ukraine BIT (1994) had entered into force, showing that the incorporation was not undertaken to gain access to ICSID arbitration.[77]

Figure 4. Investment by an investor from a non-Contracting Party through an intermediate company established in the Contracting Party

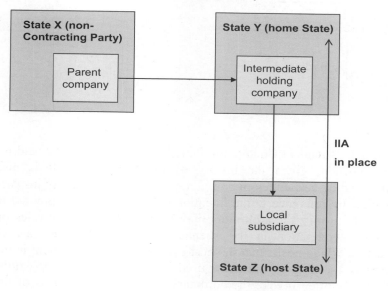

This decision gave rise to a strong dissent from the President of the tribunal, Professor Prosper Weil,[78] who held that this finding undermined the object and purpose of the ICSID Convention, which required that the investor be a national of a Contracting Party other

Figure 5. Investment by an investor from the host State through an intermediate company established in the Contracting Party

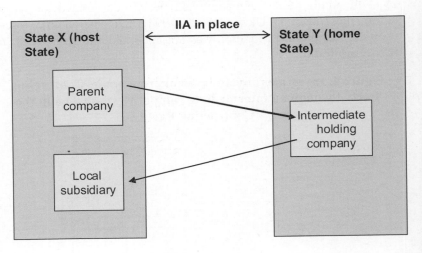

than the respondent Contracting Party. There is much to be said for this position, given the history of the Convention. It is also supported by academic opinion.[79] Against this, the majority justifies its view by reference to the intention of the parties as expressed in the BIT. In this, the arbitrators may be said to follow the rules on treaty interpretation in the Vienna Convention on the Law of Treaties, which posits that the best evidence of parties' intent is the ordinary meaning of the terms used in the treaty. In other words, arbitrators often invoke the "ordinary meaning of the terms of the treaty" and decline to infer any other "intent" because that is what the Vienna Convention calls for. It may be said, in response, that the jurisdiction of ICSID cannot be determined by the subjective intention of the parties to a BIT but by the Convention organs themselves.[80] More recently, in *TSA Spectrum de Argentina S.A. v. Argentine Republic*, the corporate veil was lifted by the tribunal to reveal that the Dutch claimant company was in fact owned and controlled by an Argentine citizen for the purposes of Article 25(2)(b) of the ICSID Convention and so the tribunal had no jurisdiction.[81] Thus, the approach of the majority in the *Tokios Tokelés* case is not uniformly followed, though a number of more recent cases have done so where the applicable treaty and/or national law refer only to a test of formal incorporation as determining nationality.[82]

The formal approach to corporate nationality as a factor in determining personal jurisdiction in *Tokios Tokelés* has been applied in other arbitrations. It has been held that where the local subsidiary is controlled by a company established in a non-Contracting Party, but where the ultimate parent is incorporated in a Contracting Party, ICSID will have jurisdiction over a claim brought by the parent (see figure 6). The nationality of the intermediate holding company will not be decisive.[83] Thus, in Company X v. State A, State A objected to ICSID jurisdiction based on the fact that, notwithstanding its apparent consent to jurisdiction under Art. 25(2)(b), the immediate controller of the local subsidiary, Company X, had the nationality of a state not party to the Convention and so the requirements of Art. 25(2)(b) were not met. The tribunal rejected this argument on the ground that since the immediate controller was itself controlled by nationals of a Contracting State, Company X was entitled to bring ICSID proceedings, it having the nationality of those foreign controllers for the purpose of Art. 25(2)(b).[84]

**Figure 6. Investment through an intermediate company
incorporated in a non-Contracting Party**

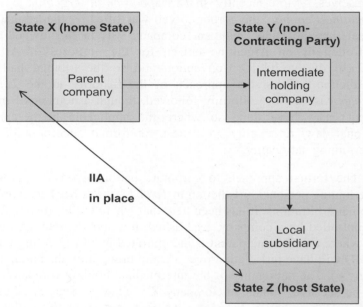

A similar position has been taken in relation to NAFTA claims. In *Waste Management v. Mexico*, a United States corporation claimed against Mexico for losses suffered by its Mexican subsidiary, which was owned through two Cayman Islands corporations, arising out of operations concerning a landfill site in Mexico. The tribunal held that, as NAFTA was not restricted to claimants having the nationality of one or other of the Contracting Parties, and given that the Mexican enterprise was indirectly controlled by the United States claimant, the nationality of the intermediate holding companies was irrelevant.[85] Equally, as held in the case of *Autopista v. Venezuela*, where the directly controlling parent is a national of a non-Contracting Party, and this fact is known to the host country, a subsequent transfer of a majority of its shares in the local subsidiary to an intermediate holding company possessing the nationality of a Contracting Party, will not be fatal to ICSID jurisdiction, where the host Contracting Party is aware of the situation and has applied a formal test of nationality to the local subsidiary (Muchlinski 2007, p. 730; Schlemmer 2008, p. 60).[86]

More recently, in the case of *Rompetrol v. Romania*, the tribunal rejected the respondent State's argument that, notwithstanding the fact that the claimant's formal nationality met the requirements of the applicable BIT, both the BIT and the ICSID Convention required an investigation of the actual control over a corporate claimant to establish nationality.[87] The claimant was incorporated in the Netherlands. The dispute arose from the claimant's investment in the Romanian oil sector and, in particular, the purchase of shares by the claimant in Rompetrol Rafinare S.A. (RRC), a privatized Romanian company which owns and operates an oil refinery and petrochemical complex. The claimant alleged that the Romanian Government ordered "extraordinary and unreasonable" investigations of RRC and its management, as well as "discriminatory and arbitrary" treatment of the company, which according to the claimant amounted to violations of the Netherlands-Romania BIT (1994).[88] The respondent argued that as the ultimate controller of the claimant was a Romanian national it could not bring a claim under the BIT. The tribunal held that the BIT contained a test of formal nationality by way of incorporation for legal persons that was entirely consistent with the *Barcelona Traction Case*. In the circumstances it was not necessary to read into the agreement a control-based "effective link" test of nationality or to examine the factual basis of the assertion that the claimant company was in fact under Romanian control.

Similarly, in the case of *Rumeli v. Kazakhstan*, the tribunal was faced with an allegation that the claimant was no more than a shell company with the real controlling interest vesting in the Turkish State and not in an investor who was a national of Turkey, the other Contracting State in the Kazakhstan-Turkey BIT (1992) under which the claim was made. The tribunal dismissed this argument on the basis that *"[t]he BIT does not provide a basis for looking beyond a company on the alleged basis that it would be a shell company and does not exclude such companies from its scope of application from the moment it is incorporated in another contracting State"*.[89]

In sum, both intermediate holding companies and ultimate parent companies have rights to bring a claim on the basis of their investment in the subsidiary company located in the host country. If they possess the nationality of a Contracting Party other than the host country, they are also "investors" who can bring a claim. The *Tokios Tokelés* case shows that "treaty shopping" is a phenomenon that tribunals will accept if they take a formal view of a BIT that makes the nationality of incorporation the main test of nationality for a legal entity to be regarded as an "investor". Equally, the use of an intermediate holding company in a non-Contracting Party has also been seen as no bar to jurisdiction, nor has the ownership of the local subsidiary by a non-Contracting Party parent company, which then transfers the majority of the shares in the subsidiary to a holding company in a Contracting Party. This paves the way for investors to structure their investments so as to take advantage of nominal "home" jurisdictions that have a network of BITs in place so as to attract "treaty shoppers". However, a State may not see this as a problem if it considers irrelevant whether the capital originates from a Contracting Party or from a non-Contracting Party. In other words, a country's negotiation position may be based on a view that an IIA achieves its purpose as long as it attracts foreign capital, and that the country of the capital's origin is of little importance.

(c) Denial-of-benefits clause

To limit treaty shopping, certain BITs use a "denial of benefits" clause. Thus, the model BIT (2004) used by the United States, which also uses country-of-organization as the test of nationality, permits the host country to refuse to extend treaty benefits to investments owned by investors of the other Party if the investors do not have substantial business activities in the territory of the other Party or if the country of ultimate control does not have normal economic relations with the host country. For example, Article 17 of the Rwanda-United States BIT (2008) provides that:

> *"1. A Party may deny the benefits of this Treaty to an investor of the other Party that is an enterprise of such other Party and to investments of that investor if persons of a non-Party own or control the enterprise and the denying Party:*
> *(a) does not maintain diplomatic relations with the non-Party; or*
> *(b) adopts or maintains measures with respect to the non-Party or a person of the non-Party that prohibit transactions with the enterprise or that would be violated or circumvented if the benefits of this Treaty were accorded to the enterprise or to its investments.*
> *2. A Party may deny the benefits of this Treaty to an investor of the other Party that is an enterprise of such other Party and to investments of that investor **if the enterprise has no substantial business activities in the territory of the other Party and persons of a non-Party, or of the denying Party, own or control the enterprise.**"* (Emphasis added.)

This introduces a twofold test for avoiding treaty shopping. First, it allows the tribunal to determine if the investor has any substantial business activities in the home country. This requires some analysis of what constitutes "substantial business activities". Some guidance could be obtained here from municipal law rules as to business presence for the purposes of jurisdiction over foreign companies. Normally, this would require more than a "brass plate" office with an address for legal service and evidence of some clear business activity in the jurisdiction. Similarly, taxation laws that seek to distinguish between income located abroad for tax deferral purposes and genuine manufacturing activities for the purposes of so-called "controlled foreign corporations" rules could offer some guidance (Muchlinski 2007, pp 141, 303).

The second part of the test is one of ownership or control, which introduces a veil-lifting possibility: a denying Party (host State) can lift the corporate veil to determine the owners or controllers of the alleged "investor". If such owner/controller originates from a third State or from the host State itself, treaty protection can be denied. For example, in *Banro American Resources et al. v. Congo*, a Canadian parent company sought diplomatic protection, as a national of a non-Contracting State, against the Congo, and its United States subsidiary, which undertook the actual investment in that country, sought to file a claim before ICSID. The tribunal rejected jurisdiction on the ground that it was not open to the group to neutralize the nationality requirements of the ICSID Convention in this way and to undermine the fundamental consensual characteristic of the Convention between the host Contracting State and the home Contracting State of which the foreign investor is a national.[90]

A denial of benefits clause can be formulated as discretionary ("a Party may deny the benefits" or "a Party reserves a right to deny the advantages") or automatic ("benefits shall be denied"). Early arbitral practice reviewed below shows that the language used in the denial of benefits does matter, and that it may be difficult to use a discretionary clause in an effective way (see Section II.B.(2)(d)).

In addition, it is not certain that the approach in *Tokios Tokelés* could be uniformly followed. For example, the tribunal in the NAFTA case of *Loewen v. United States* suggested that, under NAFTA, for an international claim to be sustainable, diversity of nationality must exist between the claimant investor and the respondent State from the date of the inception of the claim to the date of resolution. Accordingly, where, as in that case, the reorganization of the claimant company, due to its bankruptcy, caused it to lose its original Canadian nationality and to acquire United States nationality, the international character of the claim disappeared.[91] The absence of any evidence that its controller, a Canadian national, retained any shares in the reorganized company was fatal to any personal claim he might have had under NAFTA.[92] It should be noted that this is a NAFTA case and is not binding upon an ICSID tribunal determining jurisdiction under any other IIA. In addition, as noted above, under Article 25(2)(b), diversity of nationality need only exist under the ICSID Convention at the date the parties consent to the claim being brought and not at the date of its resolution. However, the decision in Loewen does stress the need to maintain a distinction between disputes of a purely national character, which should be settled before national bodies, and genuine international disputes (Muchlinski 2007, p. 730).

(d) Denial of benefits under the Energy Charter Treaty

The denial of benefits clause in Article 17(1) of the Energy Charter Treaty (ECT) has been interpreted in several arbitral awards. By Article 17 of the ECT:

> *"Each Contacting Party reserves the right to deny the advantages of this Part to:*
> *(1) a legal entity if citizens or nationals of a third state own or control such entity and if that entity has no substantial business activities in the Area of the Contracting Party in which it is organized; [...]*
> *(2) an Investment, if the denying Contracting Party establishes that such Investment is an Investment of an Investor of a third state with or as to which the denying Contracting Party:*
> > *(a) does not maintain a diplomatic relationship; or*
> > *(b) adopts or maintains measures that:*

> *(i) prohibit transactions with Investors of that state; or*
> *(ii) would be violated or circumvented if the benefits of*
> *this Part were accorded to Investors of that state or to*
> *their Investments.*" (Emphasis added.)

It must be noted that Article 17(1) refers to owners and controllers only from a third State but *not* from the host State. This is a peculiar approach that leaves a loophole for domestic investors from the host State to benefit from the ECT protection if they structure their investment through a territory of another Contracting Party. Also, this provision has to be read together with the definition of "Investor" in Article 1(7). According to the tribunal in *AMTO v. Ukraine*, this provision establishes two classes of investors of a Contracting Party for the purposes of the ECT:

> "*The first class comprises Investors with an indefeasible right to investment protection under the ECT. This class includes nationals of another Contracting Party – whether natural persons or juridical entities – except for those nationals falling within the second class.*
>
> *The second class comprises Investors that have a defeasible right to investment protection under the ECT, because the host State of the investment has the power to divest the Investor of this right. In this second class are legal entities that satisfy the nationality requirement by reason of incorporation but are owned or controlled by nationals of a third state in a manner potentially unacceptable to the host State. Such foreign ownership or control is potentially unacceptable where it involves a State with which the Host State does not maintain normal diplomatic or economic relationships, or where it is not accompanied by substantial business activity in the state of incorporation.*"[93]

The tribunal went on to assert that:

"Article 17(1) affects only juridical rather than natural persons, and requires the fulfilment of two requirements in order for the host state to exercise its right to deny. First, the investor must be owned or controlled by citizens or nationals of a 'third state'. 'Third state' is not defined in the ECT, but is used in Article 1(7) in contradistinction to 'Contracting Party', which suggests that a third state is any state that is not a Contracting Party to the ECT. Secondly, the investor must have 'no substantial business activities' in the state of its incorporation. These are cumulative requirements so that both must exist before the respondent can exercise its right to deny."[94]

On the facts of this case, the question arose whether the claimant company should be denied the protection of the ECT on the grounds that it was ultimately controlled by Russian nationals, the Russian Federation being a signatory of the ECT but not having ratified the treaty. The tribunal rejected this argument. AMTO was a limited liability company incorporated in Latvia, a full party to the ECT, whose shares were owned by a Lichtenstein holding company that was itself controlled by a Lichtenstein-based foundation, and thus a national of another Contracting Party. The controller of the foundation was indeed a Russian citizen but that was not conclusive proof that AMTO could not benefit from the protection of the ECT, especially as the Russian Federation's status as a "third State" was a complex matter, given that it had signed the ECT. However, that issue did not have to be decided as the decisive fact was that AMTO *"has substantial business activity in Latvia, on the basis of its investment related activities conducted from premises in Latvia, and involving the employment of a small but permanent staff"*.[95]

This award is notable for the determination that the test of substantial business activity can be relatively easily met in that it does not require large-scale or extensive operations in the host contracting State, but it is questionable if other tribunals applying

Article 17 could so easily ignore the issue of third state control. Other awards have clearly stated that both parts of Article 17(1) have to be given equal weight.[96]

Problems relating to invocation of the clause. The denial-of-benefits clause is formulated in the ECT as discretionary (a "Party reserves the right to deny..."). At least two arbitral tribunals have held that such formulation allows a State to deny the protections of the treaty only prospectively, not retrospectively.[97] In other words, according to these tribunals, a State cannot deny the benefits of the treaty to an investor after the claim is brought, in relation to events that took place before the initiation of proceedings. This interpretation would seem to impose on a host State a task of denying benefits to non-qualifying investors at an early stage. In practice, this seems to mean that a government is supposed to monitor ultimate owners and controllers of all incoming investments (who can also change over time), as well as determine whether the direct owner engages in substantial economic activity in the territory of the other contracting party. Such an approach is unfeasible in practice and would seem to deprive the clause of much of its useful effect. Arguably, however, even under this "prospective" interpretation, a State may deny the benefits of the treaty (including the investor's right to initiate international arbitral proceedings) *after* the investor notifies the State of the dispute but before he submits the claim to arbitration. This is because the consent to arbitration is perfected by the investor only at the latter moment. This reading would give States some time to investigate the nationality of the company's owners/controllers and to see whether the company carries out substantial business activities in the country of incorporation.

Even though it may be too early to say that the case law on this point is settled,[98] it may be more prudent to formulate a denial-of-benefits clause as automatic ("benefits shall be denied"). Another way to deal with the problem may be to issue a declaration (or attach it to the treaty at the time of conclusion) expressly denying the benefits of the IIA (or IIAs) to all those investors that fall within the ambit of the clause.

(e) Implications for treaty negotiation

The above cases on corporate nationality suggest that more attention needs to be paid in the drafting of definitions of "investor" to actual foreign control and to the possibility of treaty shopping that a formal reading of place of incorporation test creates. For this purpose, negotiators may consider supplementing the country-of-organization test with the company-seat test and/or requirement of real or substantial economic activities in the home State, and/or a denial-or-benefits clause (discretionary or automatic). On the other hand, if a government is willing to grant IIA protection to investments regardless of whether they flow from the other Contracting Party, from a third State or even from its own territory (channelled through the territory of the other Contracting Party), the country-of-organization test will suffice.

C. Territory

Investment generally is covered by an investment agreement only if it is in the territory of one of the State parties to the agreement. Some investment agreements define the term "territory". The most common definition is typified by Article 1 (4) of the Lebanon-Republic of Korea BIT (2006), which provides that,

"'Territory' means the territory of the Contracting Parties, including the territorial sea as well as the maritime areas including the exclusive economic zone, its seabed and subsoil adjacent to the outer limit of the territorial sea over which the State concerned exercises, in accordance with national and international law, jurisdiction and sovereign rights."

The Energy Charter Treaty (1994) provides a similar definition in Article 1, para. (10):

> *"'Area' means with respect to a state that is a Contracting Party:*
> *the territory under its sovereignty, it being understood that territory includes land, internal waters and the territorial sea; and*
> *subject to and in accordance with the international law of the sea: the sea, sea-bed and its subsoil with regard to which that Contracting Party exercises sovereign rights and jurisdiction."*

As is evident, the purpose of the definition of "territory" generally is not to describe the land territory of the parties, but to indicate that "territory" includes maritime zones over which the host country exercises jurisdiction. The significance is that investments located within the host country's maritime jurisdiction, such as mineral exploration or extraction facilities, would be covered by the agreement. More recent agreements have included such comprehensive definitions of territory emphasizing the wider area of control that current international law gives to states in relation to the extraction of natural resources in particular (UNCTAD 2007a, pp. 18-19).

Even where it is completely clear which geographical areas constitute the territory of a party, there may still be uncertainty concerning whether an investment is located in the territory of a party. Because "investment" includes many intangible rights, the location of a particular asset may be difficult to identify. For example, a service provider in one country may sign an agreement with a company headquartered in a second country to perform professional services for a branch of the company in a third country. The definition of "investment" may well include the rights derived from that contract, but it may be unclear which of the three countries should be considered the location of the "investment" of contractual rights. The texts of IIAs, however, provide little assistance in resolving issues concerning the location of investments.

Notes

[1] In the General Agreement on Trade in Services (GATS) "commercial presence" is defined as meaning *"any type of business or professional establishment, including through (i) the constitution, acquisition or maintenance of a juridical person, or (ii) the creation or maintenance of a branch or a representative office within the territory of a Party for the purpose of supplying a service"* (Article XXVIII(d)).

[2] As noted by Westcott, *"by limiting the treaty's coverage of investment to commercial presence, an important narrowing is assured. The constitution, acquisition or maintenance of a business, professional establishment or branch for the purpose of economic activity is a much more limited concept than commonly used asset-based definitions of investment that cover portfolio investments and a range of other assets such as intellectual property."* (Westcott 2008, p. 9).

[3] See further, UNCTAD 2005b.

[4] See, for example, CARIFORUM-EU EPA (2008), Title II, Chapter 2 "Commercial presence".

[5] Another alternative to the asset-based approach is to omit the reference to assets generally and to include instead an enumeration of the transactions covered (see, e.g. the OECD Code of Liberalisation of Capital Movements, which does not define the term "investment" or "capital" as such, but contains in Annex A lists of capital movements to be liberalized, including direct investment). The transaction-based definition is conceptually different from the asset-based definition as the former necessarily considers only the transaction of establishing or liquidating an investment, not the protection of assets. Thus, it would only be suitable for those agreements that are limited to liberalization of investment.

6   Unless otherwise noted, all instruments and BITs' texts cited in this report may be found in UNCTAD's online collection of BITs and IIAs at www.unctad.org/iia.

7   Agreement between the Government of the United Kingdom of Great Britain and Northern Ireland and the Government of the United Mexican States for the Promotion and Reciprocal Protection of Investments, 2006.

8   This agreement has been superseded by the ASEAN Comprehensive Investment Agreement (2009), which did not retain this exclusion.

9   The 10% benchmark is used in the IMF Balance of Payments Manual (IMF 1993), para. 362, and the OECD Benchmark Definition of Foreign Direct Investment (OECD 1996), para. 7.

10   See, for example, Japan–Singapore EPA (2002), Article 72(a)(v).

11   See Canada–Colombia FTA, Article 838, footnote 11.

12   See Peru–United States FTA (2006), Annex 10-F "Public Debt" and the definition of "negotiated restructuring" in Article 10.28 "Definitions".

13   *Phoenix Action Ltd v. Czech Republic*, ICSID Case No. ARB/06/5, Award, 15 April 2009, para. 142.

14   See for example Benin–China BIT (2004).

15   *Phoenix Action Ltd v. Czech Republic*, ICSID Case No. ARB/06/5, Award, 15 April 2009, para. 103.

16   See, for example, *Fraport AG Frankfurt Airport Services Worldwide v. The Philippines*, ICSID Case No. Arb/03/25, Award, 16 August 2007. (Jurisdiction refused where the claimant had deliberately sought to evade nationality of ownership requirements under local law and where the Germany-Philippines BIT required that investments be made in accordance with the laws of the Philippines.)

17   *Plama Consortium Limited v. Bulgaria*, ICSID Case No. Arb/03/24, Award, 27 August 2008, paras. 138-139; *Phoenix Action Ltd v. Czech Republic*, ICSID Case No. ARB/06/5, Award, 15 April 2009, para. 101.

18   *Phoenix Action Ltd v. Czech Republic*, ICSID Case No. ARB/06/5, Award, 15 April 2009, para. 109; *Inceysa Vallisoletana, S.L. v.*

Republic of El Salvador, ICSID Case No. ARB/03/26, Award, 2 August 2006, paras. 239, 245-252.

19 *Ioannis Kardassopoulos v. Georgia,* ICSID Case No. ARB/05/18, Decision on Jurisdiction, 6 July 2007, para. 182.

20 *Desert Line Projects LLC v. Yemen,* ICSID Case No. ARB/05/17, Award, 6 February 2008.

21 Ibid., para. 106.

22 Ibid., para. 119.

23 See *Salini Costruttori SpA and Italstrade Spa v. Kingdom of Morocco,* ICSID Case No. ARB/00/4, Decision on Jurisdiction, 23 July 2001 (42 *International Legal Materials* 609 (2003)), para. 46; *Tokios Tokelés v. Ukraine,* ICSID Case No. ARB/02/18, Decision on Jurisdiction, 29 April 2004 (20 *ICSID Review-Foreign Investment Law Journal* 205 (2005)), para. 84.

24 *Fedax v. Venezuela,* ICSID Case No. Arb/96/3, Decision on Jurisdiction, 11 July 1997 (37 *International Legal Materials* 1378 (1998)), para. 43: *"The basic features of an investment have been described as involving a certain duration, a certain regularity of profit and return, assumption of risk, a substantial commitment and a significance for the host states development."*

25 *Pantechniki S.A. Contractors & Engineers v. Albania,* ICSID Case No. ARB/07/21, Award, 30 July 2009, paras. 46-49.

26 *Romak S.A v. Uzbekistan,* PCA Case No. AA280, Award, 26 November 2009, para. 207.

27 Ibid., paras. 242-243.

28 As noted by the tribunal in *Desert Line Projects LLC v. Yemen,* ICSID Case No. ARB/05/17, Award, 6 February 2008, para. 110.

29 For example, Article II(2) of the Argentina-Spain BIT (1991) states: *"This agreement shall not however apply to disputes or claims arising before entry into force."* This provision was relied upon by Spain to contest jurisdiction in the case of *Maffezini v. Spain,* ICSID Case No. Arb/97/7, Decision on Objections to Jurisdiction, 25 January 2000 (16 *ICSID Review-Foreign Investment Law Journal* 212 (2001)). Spain

argued that the dispute, which concerned compliance with environmental law requirements by the claimant, had arisen before the entry into force of the treaty in 1992. This was not accepted by the Tribunal which upheld jurisdiction.

[30] *Bayindir v. Pakistan*, ICSID Case No. Arb/03/29, Decision on Jurisdiction, 14 November 2005, para. 131.

[31] See also for example, Indonesia–Japan EPA (2007), Article 58.

[32] *Ceskoslovenska Obchodni Banka, A.S. v. The Slovak Republic*, Decision on Jurisdiction, 24 May 1999 (14 *ICSID Review-Foreign Investment Law Journal* 251 (1999)).

[33] *Joy Mining v. Egypt*, ICSID Case No. ARB/03/11, Decision on Jurisdiction, 6 August 2004, para. 45. Note that in *X (United Kingdom) v. The Republic (Central Europe)*, SCC Case 49/2002, a "best efforts" agreement to secure necessary licenses for the investment did not have a financial value and so could not be an "investment" under the applicable BIT.

[34] *Joy Mining v. Egypt*, ICSID Case No. ARB/03/11, Decision on Jurisdiction, 6 August 2004, para. 52.

[35] *Mihaly v. Sri Lanka*, ICSID Case No.ARB/00/2, Award, 15 March 2002 (41 *International Legal Materials* 867 (2002)), paras. 51-60. Here, the claimant sought to recover preliminary expenditure undertaken by it in preparation for a build–operate–transfer (BOT) contract to construct a power station in the respondent State. That contract was ultimately never concluded. Also, in the separate concurring opinion of Mr David Suratgar, it was asserted that pre-contractual expenditure by a subsidiary in a BOT contract should in principle be seen as an "investment", even if it is not incurred by reason of a signed contract but in anticipation of such signature. See *Mihaly v. Sri Lanka*, ICSID Case No.ARB/00/2, Award and Concurring Opinion, 15 March 2002 (41 *International Legal Materials* 867 (2002)), pp. 878–880.

[36] *PSEG v. Turkey*, ICSID Case No. ARB/02/5. Decision on Jurisdiction, 4 June 2004 (44 *International Legal Materials* 465 (2005)), para. 88.

[37] See further *Mytilineos Holdings SA v. The State Union of Serbia & Montenegro and Republic of Serbia,* UNCITRAL, Partial Award, 8

September 2006, paras. 117–125. The *ad hoc* tribunal, though holding that it was not required to follow ICSID requirements as to subject matter jurisdiction, still analyzed the facts on the basis of such requirements as they had been put in argument to the tribunal. See also *Romak* S.A *v. Uzbekistan,* PCA Case No. AA280, Award, 26 November 2009.

[38] *Joy Mining v. Egypt,* ICSID Case No. ARB/03/11, Decision on Jurisdiction, 6 August 2004, para. 53. See also *Bayindir v. Pakistan,* ICSID Case No. Arb/03/29, Decision on Jurisdiction, 14 November 2005, paras. 122-138; *Jan de Nul v. Egypt,* ICSID Case No. Arb/04/13, Decision on Jurisdiction, 16 June 2006, paras. 90-96; *Saipem Spa v. Bangladesh,* ICSID Case No. ARB/05/7, Decision on Jurisdiction, 21 March 2007, paras. 99-114; *Ioannis Kardassopoulos v. Georgia,* ICSID Case No. ARB/05/18, Decision on Jurisdiction, 6 July 2007, para. 116.

[39] *Phoenix Action Ltd v. Czech Republic,* ICSID Case No. ARB/06/5, Award, 15 April 2009, para. 114.

[40] Ibid., para. 34.

[41] Ibid., paras. 143-145.

[42] *Global Trading Resource v. Ukraine,* ICSID Case No. ARB/09/11, Award of 1 December 2010, paras. 56-58.

[43] *Romak S.A v. Uzbekistan,* PCA Case No. AA280, Award, 26 November 2009, para. 207 (emphasis in original).

[44] Ibid., para. 222.

[45] Ibid., para. 227.

[46] Ibid., para. 232.

[47] Ibid., para. 230.

[48] *Biwater v. Tanzania,* ICSID Case No. ARB/05/22, Award, 24 July 2008, para. 312. See too *Rompetrol v. Romania,* ICSID Case No. ARB/06/3, Decision on Jurisdiction, 18 April 2008, para.107: *"At a deeper level, though, the Tribunal is not persuaded that there is anything in the rules of treaty interpretation that would justify giving*

the ICSID Convention overriding effect for the interpretation of the BIT."

49   See *Saluka Investments BV v. Czech Republic,* UNCITRAL, Partial Award, 17 March 2006, paras. 209-211. See also *LESI-Dipenta v. Algeria,* ICSID Case No. ARB/03/8, Decision on Jurisdiction, 12 July 2006, para. 72(iv).

50   *Victor Pey Casado and President Allende Foundation v. Republic of Chile,* ICSID Case No. ARB/98/2, Award, 8 May 2008, para. 232 (unofficial translation from French).

51   *Malaysian Historical Salvors v. Malaysia,* ICSID Case No. ARB/05/10, Annulment Decision, 16 April 2009.

52   *Malaysian Historical Salvors v. Malaysia,* ICSID Case No. ARB/05/10, Award, 17 May 2007, para. 143:

53   By Article 1 *"For the purpose of this Agreement (1)(a) 'investment' means every kind of asset and in particular, though not exclusively, includes:* […] *(ii) shares, stock and debentures of companies or interests in the property of such companies; (iii) claims to money or to any performance under contract having a financial value; (iv) intellectual property rights* […]*; (v) business concessions conferred* […] *under contract* […]*".*

54   *Malaysian Historical Salvors v. Malaysia,* ICSID Case No. ARB/05/10, Annulment Decision, 16 April 2009, para. 60.

55   Ibid., para. 80.

56   *Malaysian Historical Salvors v. Malaysia,* ICSID Case No. ARB/05/10, Dissenting Opinion, 16 April 2009, para. 22.

57   Ibid., paras. 43–47.

58   *CMS Gas Transmission Co v. Argentina,* ICSID Case No. ARB/01/8, Decision on Jurisdiction, 17 July 2003 (42 *International Legal Materials* 788 (2003)), para. 51.

59   *Lauder v. Czech Republic,* UNCITRAL, Final Award, 3 September 2001.

60   *CME Czech Republic v. Czech Republic,* UNCITRAL, Final Award, 14 March 2003.

61   Ibid., para. 436.

[62] *Nottebohm Case (Liechtenstein v. Guatemala)*, ICJ, Judgement, 18 November 1953; Judgement, 6 April 1955 (*International Court of Justice Reports*, 1955, pp. 4-65).

[63] *Nottebohm Case (Liechtenstein v. Guatemala)*, ICJ, Judgement, 18 November 1953; Judgement, 6 April 1955 (*ICJ Reports*, 1955, pp. 4-65); *Barcelona Traction, Light and Power Company, Limited (Belgium v. Spain)*, ICJ, 1970, Judgement, 24 July 1964; Judgement, 5 February 1970 (*ICJ Reports*, 1970, pp. 3-357).

[64] *Champion Trading Company and others v. Arab Republic of Egypt*, ICSID No. Arb/02/9, Decision on Jurisdiction, 21 October 2003; *Waguih Elie George Siag and Clorinda Vecchi v. The Arab Republic of Egypt*, ICSID Case No. Arb/05/15, Decision on Jurisdiction, 11 April 2007; *Hussein Nuaman Soufraki v. The United Arab Emirates*, ICSID Case No. Arb/02/7, Award, 7 July 2004. For criticism of this position see Schlemmer 2008.

[65] *Micula v. Romania*, ICSID Case No. ARB/05/20, Decision on Jurisdiction and Admissibility, 24 September 2008.

[66] *Hussein Nuaman Soufraki v. The United Arab Emirates*, ICSID Case No. Arb/02/7 7, Award, July 2004.

[67] *Ibid.*, para. 83.

[68] *Barcelona Traction, Light and Power Company, Limited (Belgium v. Spain)*, ICJ, 1970, Judgement, 24 July 1964; Judgement, 5 February 1970 (*ICJ Reports*, 1970, pp. 3-357).

[69] The most recent version of the German model BIT (2008) has a different definition of "company", revised to conform to the law of the European Union.

[70] *Vacuum Salt v. Ghana*, ICSID Case No. ARB/92/1, Award, 16 February 1994 (9 *ICSID Review-Foreign Investment Law Journal* 72 (1994)). These summaries are taken from Muchlinski 2007, pp.728-729.

[71] *Ibid.*, para. 36.

[72] *Ibid.*, para. 53

[73] *Aguas del Tunari v. Bolivia*, ICSID Case No. ARB/02/3, Decision on Jurisdiction, 21 October 2005 (20 *ICSID Review-Foreign Investment Law Journal* 450 (2005)), paras. 206-232.

[74] *Tokios Tokelés v. Ukraine*, ICSID Case No. ARB/02/18, Decision on Jurisdiction, 29 April 2004 (20 *ICSID Review-Foreign Investment Law Journal* 205 (2005)).

[75] *Ibid.*, paras. 45–51. See also *Saluka Investments BV v. Czech Republic*, UNCITRAL, Partial Award, 17 March 2006.The Tribunal held that a formal legal definition of "investor" is effective to determine corporate nationality and that, in the absence of a specific treaty provision, a Tribunal does not have the power to look behind corporate structures unless these have been used to perpetrate fraud or other malfeasance (paras. 229-230).

[76] *Ibid.*, para. 52.

[77] *Ibid.*, para. 56.

[78] *Tokios Tokelés v. Ukraine*, ICSID Case No. ARB/02/18, Dissenting Opinion, 29 April 2004 (20 *ICSID Review-Foreign Investment Law Journal* 245 (2005)).

[79] Thus, Schreuer et al. 2009, p. 323, para. 849 asserts: "*the better approach would appear to be a realistic look at the true controllers thereby blocking access to the Centre for juridical persons that are controlled directly or indirectly by nationals of non-Contracting States or nationals of the host State*".

[80] *Tokios Tokelés v. Ukraine*, ICSID Case No. ARB/02/18, Dissenting Opinion, 29 April 2004 (20 *ICSID Review-Foreign Investment Law Journal* 245 (2005)), para. 16.

[81] *TSA Spectrum de Argentina S.A. v. Argentine Republic*, ICSID Case No. ARB/05/5, Award, 19 December 2008, paras. 114-162.

[82] See *ADC v. Hungary*, ICSID Case No. ARB/03/16, Award, 2 October 2006, para. 360; *Rompetrol v. Romania*, ICSID Case No. ARB/06/3, Decision on Jurisdiction, 18 April 2008, para. 85.

[83] *SOABI v. Senegal*, ICSID Case ARB/82/1, Decision on Jurisdiction, 1 August 1984 (2 *ICSID Reports* 175), pp. 182–183.

[84] *Company X v. State A*, *News from ICSID*, Vol. 2 No. 2, Summer 1985, pp. 3–6.

[85] *Waste Management v. Mexico*, ICSID Case No. ARB(AF)/00/3, Award, 30 April 2004 (43 *International Legal Materials* 967 (2004)), paras. 77, 80 and 85.

[86] *Autopista v. Venezuela*, ICSID Case No. ARB/00/5, Decision on Jurisdiction, 27 September 2001, (16 *ICSID Review-Foreign Investment Law Journal* 469 (2001)). Venezuela had permitted a Mexican parent to transfer 75 per cent of its shares in its local subsidiary to a United States affiliate, which then became the direct owner of the subsidiary. The tribunal held that it had jurisdiction to hear a claim brought by the United States affiliate as Venezuela had applied a simple majority shareholding test for determining foreign nationality, and it was not open to it to challenge this choice by reference to economic criteria even if they would better reflect reality (paras. 117–122) There was no evidence that the United States affiliate was a corporation of convenience. The transfer was necessary to ensure access to adequate capital during the Mexican Peso crisis (paras. 123–126) The fact that Mexico, a non-Contracting Party, had taken an interest in the dispute at the diplomatic level was not fatal to the claim by the United States affiliate (paras. 135-140). The *Banro Case* was distinguished as the transfer of the shares in that case was not subject to the approval of the Government and the parties had not defined the test of foreign control, see *Banro American Resources et al. v. Congo*, ICSID Case ARB/98/7, Award, 1 September 2000 (excerpts) (17 *ICSID Review-Foreign Investment Law Journal* 382 (2002)), para. 143.

[87] *Rompetrol v. Romania*, ICSID Case No. ARB/06/3, Decision on Jurisdiction, 18 April 2008, para. 78.

[88] Ibid., para. 3.

[89] *Rumeli Telekom a.s. and Telsim Mobil Telekomikasyon Hizmetleri a.s v. Republic of Kazakhstan*, ICSID Case No. ARB/05/16, Award, 29 July 2008, para. 326..

[90] *Banro American Resources et al. v. Congo*, ICSID Case ARB/98/7, Award, 1 September 2000 (excerpts) (17 *ICSID Review-Foreign Investment Law Journal* 382 (2002)), paras. 11-12.

[91] *Loewen v. United States*, ICSID Case No.ARB(AF)/98/3, Award, 26 June 2003 (42 *International Legal Materials* 811 (2003)), paras. 223, 255, 232-234.

[92] *Ibid.*, para. 239. In *EnCana v. Ecuador*, UNCITRAL, Arbitration Award of the London Court of International Arbitration, 3 February 2006, it was held that continuous nationality of ownership of the subsidiary is not required where the parent makes a claim in its own right and not on behalf of its subsidiary. So long as the nationality of the parent remains that of another Contracting Party then it qualifies as an investor of that Party (para. 128).

[93] *AMTO v. Ukraine*, Arbitration Institute of the Stockholm Chamber of Commerce, Arbitration No. 080/2005, Award of 26 March 2008, para. 61.

[94] *Ibid.*, para. 62.

[95] *Ibid.*, para. 69.

[96] See *Plama Consortium Limited v. Bulgaria*, ICSID Case No. Arb/03/24, Decision on Jurisdiction, 8 February 2005 (44 *International Legal Materials* 721 (2005)), Award, 27 August 2008.

[97] *Ibid.*, paras.161-162; *Veteran Petroleum Limited (Cyprus) v. The Russian Federation*, UNCITRAL, PCA Case No. AA 228, Interim Award on Jurisdiction and Admissibility, 30 November 2009, paras. 514-515.

[98] The described interpretation may be a result of particular structure of the ECT. Under the ECT, a Contracting Part may deny the benefits only of Part III of the Treaty, which includes substantive protections, and not the benefits of Part V, which includes an investor's right to ISDS. An interpretative outcome might be different with respect to a treaty where the denial-of-benefits clause entitles an investor to deny the protections of the treaty *as a whole*, including an investor's right of action against the State.

III. ASSESSMENT AND POLICY OPTIONS

The scope of the definitions used in an IIA will materially affect the extent of protection and the rights offered by the agreement. As an initial matter, the breadth of the definition raises a number of potential concerns entirely apart from developmental considerations. For example, the inclusion of contractual claims within the meaning of "investment" could convert government regulatory action affecting the validity of private contracts into an expropriation. The inclusion of trade-related transactions within the meaning of "investment" could result in the submission of a broad range of matters to the special investor-to-State dispute settlement mechanisms created by investment agreements. In short, the interaction of a broad definition of "investment" within the operative provisions of an agreement could result in the application of treaty rules and procedures to a great range of transactions unrelated to FDI.

This is not to say, however, that broad definitions coupled with broad substantive provisions are necessarily problematic. Ultimately, the scope of the agreement is established by the interaction between all its provisions. In order to achieve a specific policy goal, parties to an agreement can choose, for example, between:

- Narrowing a definition; or
- Narrowing one or more substantive provisions; or
- Allowing general and/or sectoral exceptions from treaty obligations; or
- Any combination of these approaches.

The terms "investment" and "investor" indicate the types of interests for which a host country must pay compensation in the event of an expropriation or breach of any other IIA provision. In recent years, the application of the terms "investment" and "investor" in international investment arbitration have led to the emergence of a number of new procedural issues related to the investor State dispute settlement process. As already noted, the wide approach to the determination of an "investment" in relation to complex corporate group structures and the determination of corporate nationality based predominantly on a formal test of incorporation, have opened the door to multiple claims arising out of the same dispute from different entities and owners in the group. Excessive reliance on the country-of-organization test for legal entities has led to the emergence of "treaty shopping" whereby a group establishes a legal presence in a country that has an investor protection agreement with the host country allowing it to benefit from protection even if the ultimate controlling interest possesses a nationality of a country that is a non-party to any such agreement with the host country (see figure 4). Similarly, nationals of the host country can benefit from lax IIA wording by setting up a legal entity in another country that has a BIT with the host country in place, and then claim against the host country through that entity (see figure 5). A third issue that has been identified above is that of the use of an intermediate holding company in a non-Contracting State by a parent from a Contracting State, in order to establish a subsidiary in the host country (see figure 6). Such an arrangement often involves a tax haven or other regulatory haven jurisdiction in which the holding company is placed to take advantage of such de-regulation for the purposes of the investment. Should the protection of the BIT between the host country and the parent country apply?

In the light of such considerations, State practice in IIAs, as well as the development dimension discussed in the Introduction to this paper, the following policy options emerge:

A. Investment

The text below describes the main policy options as well as their constitutive elements.

1. Option 1: adopting a broad asset-based definition

A broad and open-ended asset-based definition of "investment" has been adopted in general to offer a maximum of investment protection as a matter of policy, by utilizing language that can extend an agreement to new forms of investment as they emerge, without renegotiation of the agreement. The developmental concern can be stated quite simply: treaty coverage of all assets included within the definition may increase exposure to investor-State claims, lead to payments of high compensations and thus not be consistent with a country's development policy. The danger of an open-ended definition is that it may commit a host country to promoting or protecting forms of transactions and assets that the host country did not contemplate at the time it entered into an agreement and would not have agreed to include within the scope of the agreement had the issue arisen explicitly.

Equally, the broad open-ended definition denies legal precision as to the scope of agreed protection as it is merely illustrative of the types of assets that are protected. Lack of precision effectively shifts the determination of what constitutes an "investment" from Contracting States to arbitrators, while open-endedness of the definition invites an expansive interpretation. This risk is enhanced where an IIA includes in the definition words like "every asset", and a tribunal follows the guiding principle that the very purpose of the IIA is to give the maximum protection to investors and their investments.

Traditionally, States have justified the use of such an approach on the basis that maximizing investor and investment protection would allow for increased investment flows. That has not proved to be uniformly the case (UNCTAD 2009) and the more specialized nature of foreign investment has created uncertainty that such an all encompassing approach to defining investment is necessarily the best way forward. Thus more recent agreements have stressed the need for greater precision in the scope and definition clause.

2. Option 2: narrowing the definition of investment

As noted in Section II, a number of agreements have done so by way of a series of methods, using either an asset-based or an enterprise-based definition as a basis. These may be broadly grouped around (a) approaches that define protected investments on the basis of closed list definition; (b) definitions including investment risk and other objective defining criteria; and (c) specific controls and exclusions. These can be used alone or in tandem depending on the degree of narrowing sought by the agreement.

(a) Option 2(1): adopting a "closed list" definition

The closed list approach has the advantage of offering a broad but finite list of covered assets and of giving specific definitions of assets so as to make clear that the agreement does not apply to certain kinds of assets. This is an emerging trend in BITs. The major advantage of this approach is that it can give greater control to the Contracting Parties as to which types of investments are covered, as there is no room for treating the list as illustrative and thus open-ended. That may be an advantage for development planning as it gives more certainty as to the scope of the protection given under the IIA. Current practice suggests that the closed list can be very comprehensive, usually only excluding purely contractual transactions such as sales of goods or services, credit arrangements other than investment loans, or claims to money not linked to investment activities. To achieve legal precision, negotiators could consider including clarifying provisions or footnotes, which often begin "for greater certainty" or "for the avoidance of doubt", which appears in newer United States BITs.

(b) Option 2(2): including investment risk and other objective defining criteria

It was seen in Section II that in contemporary practice the definition clause contains a list of the main characteristics of an investment, *"including such characteristics as the commitment of capital or other resources, the expectation of gain or profit, or the assumption of risk."*[1] The main advantage of this formulation is that it offers certain objective criteria to guide tribunals that are based on the economic distinction between commercial and investment transactions. They would appear to require that a tribunal addresses the nature of the transaction before it in its actual economic context. This allows for a more focused scope of protection under the IIA with an emphasis on genuine investments rather than a generalized protection of any valuable asset owned and/or controlled by the investor.

It may be useful to distinguish further between economic characteristics of an investment (the ones mentioned immediately above) and characteristics that are policy-oriented, i.e. those that describe eligible investments by reference to their usefulness or desirability. The latter category includes in particular the requirement of *"contribution to economic development of the host State"* considered in the context of the development-based definition below (see option 3).

The major disadvantage of the approach based on objective factors is that it may be hard to substantiate in practice: how much capital or other resources must be committed, whether there is a minimum size of commitment that will qualify as an investment, what should be the duration of the transaction, and how investment risk is to be assessed? The main problem here is how to define risk. Risk is inherent to entrepreneurial business activity and arises both in ordinary commercial transactions and in investment transactions. Thus, some special form of risk inherent only to investments may have to be identified.

(c) Option 2(3) specific exclusions and controls

As to specific exclusions:

- As some agreements examined above show, it is possible to expressly exclude classes of transactions that are deemed to be only *commercial transactions* but not investments. Thus general sales transactions, sales of services; short-term loans and certain debt securities have been excluded in this way from some agreements.

- Apart from the listing of excluded transactions, some agreements exclude *portfolio investment* (because it may be regarded as less desirable than FDI, given that it generally does not bring with it technology transfer, training or other benefits associated with FDI). Further, portfolio investment is easily withdrawn, thus creating the potential for capital volatility in the event of economic turbulence. In addition, portfolio investment is less easily monitored than direct investment, giving rise to concerns that it may be used as a mechanism for money laundering. Exclusion of portfolio investments may offer a solution, at least partial, to the risk of multiple claims by minority shareholders. On the other hand, inclusion of portfolio investment can make a positive contribution to development. It is a potential source of capital and foreign exchange. Some investors may not wish to control an investment or even have any kind of equity position in the investment. Further, given that one traditional concern about FDI was that it permitted domestic assets to fall under the control of foreign nationals, there may be sound reasons of national interest to encourage portfolio rather than direct investment in certain enterprises.

- Some investment agreements exclude *assets of less than a certain value*, perhaps because these investments are considered too small to justify the costs of treaty coverage or perhaps because of a desire to reserve to domestic investors those parts of the economy in which small investments are likely to be made. However, the exclusion of small investments could discourage small and medium-sized investors that some developing countries may be seeking to attract, at least during certain stages of the development process (UNCTAD 1998b). In such cases, a size limitation may not be useful.

- Other investment agreements exclude *investments established prior to entry into force of an agreement*, in order to avoid bestowing a windfall on the investor. Such exclusion could be interpreted as calling into question the parties' commitment to investment promotion or protection and in exceptional cases could provide a permanent competitive advantage to investors who invest after the conclusion of the agreement.

- Investment agreements may limit the *parts of the economy* to which the agreement applies, particularly as far as entry/market access disciplines are concerned. As noted in Section II, this is the approach to definition taken by the Energy Charter Treaty and to some extent in the ASEAN Comprehensive Investment Agreement (2009).

- The scope of *IPR protection* may also have to be examined to avoid the pitfalls of an overbroad protection of IPRs in order to avoid covering those IPRs that are not protected under domestic legislation of a Contracting State nor by its international commitments. Further, consistency between the IIA and the WTO Trade-Related Aspects of Intellectual Property Rights (TRIPS) Agreement needs to be considered carefully, as countries that are also members of the WTO cannot exclude their WTO obligations in any IIA they enter into (UNCTAD 2005a, pp. 23–234).

The above analysis suggests that countries need to consider carefully the consequences of including or excluding certain types of investment in the definition of "investment". Critical considerations include the purpose(s) of the investment agreement and the precise nature of the operative provisions to which the definition is applied. In addition, it may be considered whether the definition of particular terms such as IPRs, or shares or goodwill should be governed by the national law of the host country first and only supplemented by international law. Thus, as long as the national definition of the term is consistent with the host country's existing international commitments (e.g. under the TRIPS Agreement) then the national definition could be expressly used as the basis of the IIA definition of the term.

As to controls:

• The criterion of protecting only investments made in accordance with the national laws and regulations of the host country further ensures that illegal investments are not protected. However, such a provision cannot act as a general preservation of domestic discretion over investments. In particular, a country cannot replace the treaty-based definition of investment with a purely national law-based definition. Furthermore, the requirement implies good faith on the part of the host country and so it cannot rely on such a clause to avoid treaty protection on the grounds of minor technical legal irregularities in the investment-making process. On the other hand, it may be possible to make the definition of "investment" subject to national law definitions found in the law of the host country so as to ensure that there is correspondence with what are regarded as protected investments under national law and under the applicable IIA. This is not the same as relying on national law to oust international obligations; it is using national law definitions to interpret the scope of terms in the IIA, a practice already used in relation to the definition of nationality for the purposes of determining who is a protected investor.

- In order to avoid mass claims arising out of indirect investments by complex TNC group structures, a host country may wish to ensure that a control-based test of corporate nationality is included in its IIAs so that a tribunal is enabled to lift the corporate veil and to see the nationality of the ultimate controller of the investment in question. A denial-of-benefits clause can also help to minimize the risk of multiple claims in relation to indirectly held investments. Another solution might be to require a consolidation of claims under two or more BITs in one case and to introduce such a clause into all BITs signed by the host country.

- A further possible option is to include a general "interpretation of terms" clause that specifies the approach to be taken by the tribunal in interpreting terms under the agreement. For example, such a clause may specify that an interpretation of particular terms should be sensitive to developmental objectives and concerns. General interpretation clauses are found in certain national constitutions as a guide to judicial interpretation of constitutional terms. Such a device may be worth examining in relation to the scope and definition of terms in IIAs.

3. Option 3: a development-based definition

The stress given by some arbitral awards on the contribution to economic development as a factor to consider when determining whether an investment exists offers a further possible way in which the balance between investment protection and the right of the host country to pursue legitimate policy goals can be ensured. A development-based definition is not an alternative to the options set out above; rather, it provides a supplementary element that adds a clear development policy dimension to the technical definition of investment. An IIA scope and definition clause could expressly require that in order to be protected, an investment must contribute to economic development of the host State. This would have the advantage of making clear that the policy of the treaty is not just investor and investment protection, but also the protection of the legitimate expectation of the host country that the investment will make a contribution to economic development. Preambles to IIAs routinely stress that the purpose of the treaty is to encourage economic development and the transfer of capital and technology, which is a necessary first step. However, because the Vienna Convention on the Law of Treaties prioritizes the ordinary meaning of specific substantive text over general purpose statements, the Preamble is so often ignored in favour of a broad definition provision. Narrowing and focusing the scope and definition clause towards a development-oriented definition of investment may be a way to serve development objectives by ensuring that the treaty is interpreted as a development-oriented investment protection instrument.

Equally, issues of the treatment of the least developed countries (LDCs) may require some express provision for their needs. In this connection, it may at least be considered whether an IIA is better suited to such an end as compared to a specialized development cooperation agreement, given that the latter seeks to balance the particular needs of LDCs with the modalities of economic development, including aid and investment, while IIAs cover a narrower range of interests and usually remain silent over the actual level of development of the developing country party to the agreement and of its particular needs.

A development-orientated definition of investment would no doubt be controversial: again, how would a tribunal assess a contribution to development? Would a minimum size of investment be required or would small and medium sized investments also constitute a contribution? Equally, there is the risk that a subjective assessment of the contribution made by the host country and the investor might be the only available measure thereof. How could a tribunal make an objective assessment, given its limited resources and expertise? In an adversarial setting, it would hear contradictory perceptions from each party, with the host country saying the contribution was minimal and so not protected, and the investor saying that the investment made a significant contribution and that therefore the protection of the treaty was available. While these are formidable concerns which may be best addressed by elaborating the developmental requirement further by parties to a specific treaty, the requirement even in its simplest form should still play a useful role providing legal grounds for denying protection to those investments that clearly lack contribution to development.

To ensure that this perspective is accepted by an international tribunal, it may be possible to include a provision that ensures that deference is given to the host country's understanding and evaluation of the development impact of a particular investment. In this connection, the fact that an investment has been authorized by the host country may not be conclusive proof of its development impact. Each case will turn on its own facts. What may have seemed a development-friendly investment at the outset may turn out not to be development friendly in practice. Changes in circumstances may eviscerate the investment of its development potential and may require corrective regulatory intervention by the host country. Such corrective regulation may need to be protected from IIA claims by reason of a development-oriented definition of covered investment. In this connection, it should be remembered that development is an interdisciplinary concept and not a legal term of art. Thus, a holistic approach to definition is needed, which takes into consideration not only economic impacts but also social and environmental impacts such as those included in the United Nations Millennium Development Goals.

Finally, the issue of definition of "investment" should be viewed not in isolation but together with the treaty's substantive disciplines. Other types of clauses – such as an express right to regulate clause or a general exceptions clause – may well prove effective in protecting the host country's right to regulate in furtherance of legitimate development policy goals. However, such an approach would work by way of an exception allowing for what otherwise might be seen as a prima facie breach of the IIA. Making the definition of investment conditional on a contribution to the economic development of the host country would help bring developmental concerns to the fore even before going into the substantive assessment of host country measures.

B. Investor

The definitional options in this area are, perhaps, less difficult to describe. In essence, the central issue is the choice of links with one or more Contracting Parties whereby natural and legal persons become integrated into the scheme of an investment agreement.

1. Natural persons

Usually, a nationality link is sufficient, as long as the contracting party's domestic law recognizes the individual to be a national. There do not appear to be significant development implications stemming from this matter. Where a natural person possesses dual or multiple nationalities, then an effective link criterion could be inserted into the clause. Most bilateral treaties do not follow this option. On the other hand, the insertion of other connecting factors, such as residence or domicile in the country of nationality, may ensure that an effective link can be proved on the facts. The main development implication of such a variation is to ensure that only persons with a significant involvement in the economy and society of the home country could claim the protection of an investment agreement and, therefore, to minimize "free-riding" on the basis of the nationality provisions of the agreement. As noted earlier, it may also be necessary to consider whether to prevent natural persons (or indeed legal persons as well), who are host country nationals, from incorporating a legal person in the other contracting party in order to benefit from the protection of the treaty against their own country.

2. Legal persons

Two issues need to be addressed: first the range of legal persons covered and, secondly, the links between the legal person and a contracting party to an investment agreement.

As to the first issue, one option is to have all legal persons covered. This gives maximum flexibility to investors as to the choice of the legal vehicle through which to invest in a host country. The development implications of such a "free choice of means" would centre on whether the regulatory objectives of internal law can be achieved regardless of the legal form that an investor adopts. That, in turn, depends on the nature and context of internal laws and regulations. The other option is to narrow the range of legal persons covered. This might be done where the host country has a strict regime as to the legal form that a foreign investment is permitted to take or where it may wish to exclude specific types of entities such as, e.g., sovereign wealth funds.

As to the second issue, a formal country-of-incorporation linkage may be adopted. Such a linkage is very common in investment agreements but may be difficult to apply in practice, given the complex structure of multinational corporate groups. In addition, as noted earlier, a strict link of formal nationality may encourage "treaty shopping" by investors who are non-nationals of the contracting parties, in that they can set up a shell company in a contracting country and thus benefit from its IIA network. This concern is real, especially as tribunals will generally allow the test of incorporation to govern the nationality question in such cases, given the wording of the agreement. To mitigate the risk of such outcome, a definition could require – in addition to the incorporation test – that the company's seat be located in the contracting party and/or that it engage in real or substantial economic activities in the territory of that party, or include an (automatic) denial of benefits clause.

Alternatively, a wider provision could concentrate not on the formal nationality of the legal person, but its effective nationality as exemplified by the nationality of the controlling interest. This could reduce the risk of "treaty shopping" by insisting that the corporate veil is lifted and the true controlling interest is identified. On the other hand, if a government is willing to grant IIA protection to investments regardless of whether they flow from the other Contracting Party, from a third State or even from its own territory (channeled through the territory of the other Contracting Party), the country-of-organization test will suffice.

A State may need to consider whether it is willing to recognize foreign affiliates incorporated in a host country as "investors" benefiting from an agreement and not being disbarred from bringing a claim on the basis of their host country nationality. A specific clause to this effect could be included where the right to bring a claim by a local subsidiary is to be allowed. However, affiliates may in any case be protected as "investments of the investor".

As with natural persons, the major problem to be borne in mind is not to adopt a linkage provision that would permit legal persons from non-Contracting States, or from the host State itself, to benefit from the legal protection of the agreement on a "free rider" basis. Thus the scope and definition clause needs to be considered alongside the question of whether a denial-of-benefits clause, containing a control test of corporate nationality, should be included.

* * *

Definitions of investment and investor are crucial in shaping the scope of an investment agreement. They determine economic interests, to which governments extend substantive IIA protections, as well as the range of natural and legal persons who will benefit from the treaty. Thus, to a large extent, the definitions outline the boundaries of a country's exposure to possible investor–State claims.

There is no such thing as the best definition of "investment" or "investor"; each definition is a reflection of the contacting parties' preferences and policies. The aim of this paper was to discern the implications of particular treaty approaches and wording in order to assist States in finding a formula that would suit their policy objectives. Therefore, a government needs to approach the definitional issues with a clear understanding of its negotiating goals and priorities. The definitions will no doubt keep evolving as new types of investment (e.g. carbon offset contracts) or new types of investors (e.g. sovereign wealth funds) appear.

Furthermore, it is obvious that the definitions alone cannot establish an appropriate balance between affording a sufficient degree of protection to foreign investors and preserving the vital interests of the host country, including its regulatory policy space. This fundamental goal needs to be kept in mind when drafting both the definitions and each individual substantive obligation of the investment agreement.

Note

1 It may be wiser to set out the list of characteristics as cumulative by using "and" instead of "or". This would also closer reflect the practice of investment tribunals developed in the context of Article 25 of the ICSID Convention who have held that for an investment to exist, *all* of the characteristics must be present.

REFERENCES

Asouzu, Amazou (2002). "A review and critique of arbitral awards on article 25(2) (b) of the ICSID Convention", in *Journal of World Investment*, Vol. 3, No. 3 (June), pp. 397–454.

Delaume, Georges R. (1982). "Le centre international pour le règlement des différends relatifs aux investissements (CIRDI)", in *Journal du Droit International*, Vol 109, No. 775, pp. 775-843.

_____ (1983). "ICSID arbitration and the courts", in *American Journal of International Law*, Vol. 77, No: 4, pp. 784-803.

_____ (1986). "ICSID arbitration", in Julien D. M. Lew (ed.), *Contemporary Problems in International Arbitration* (London: Queen Mary College, Centre for Commercial Law Studies), chapter 4, pp. 23-39.

Dolzer, Rudolf and Schreuer, Christoph (2008). *Principles of International Investment Law* (Oxford: Oxford University Press).

Gaillard, Emmanuel (2009). "Identify or define? Reflections on the evolution of the concept of investment in ICSID practice", in Christina Binder, Ursula Kriebaum, August Reinisch and Stephan Wittich (eds.), *International Investment Law for the 21st Century: Essays in Honour of Christoph Schreuer* (Oxford: Oxford University Press), pp. 403–416.

Gallagher, Norah and Shan, Wenhua (2009). *Chinese Investment Treaties* (Oxford: Oxford University Press).

International Bank for Reconstruction and Development (IBRD) (1965). "Convention on the Settlement of Investment Disputes between States and Nationals of Other States, and report of the Executive Directors", *International Legal Materials*, Vol. 4, No. 3 (May), pp. 524-544.

International Monetary Fund (IMF) (1993). *Balance of Payments Manual*, Fifth Edition (Washington, DC. IMF), available at: http://www.imf.org/external/np/sta/bop/bopman.pdf.

Joubin-Bret, Anna (2008). "Admission and establishment in the context of investment protection", in August Reinisch (ed.), *Standards of Investment Protection* (Oxford: Oxford University Press), pp. 9-28.

Kindleberger, Charles P (1993). *A Financial History of Western Europe* (New York: Oxford University Press).

McLachlan, Campbell, Shore, Laurence and Weiniger, Matthew (2007). *International Investment Arbitration: Substantive Principles* (Oxford: Oxford University Press).

Muchlinski, Peter T. (2007). *Multinational Enterprises and the Law. Oxford* (Oxford: Oxford University Press).

Organisation for Economic Cooperation and Development (OECD) (1996). *OECD Benchmark Definition of Foreign Direct Investment*, Third Edition (Paris: OECD); available at: http://www.oecd.org/dataoecd/10/16/2090148.pdf.

Rivas, Jose Antonio (2009). *The Colombian BIT Model: A Balanced Treaty with NAFTA, OECD and Colombian Constitutional Elements*, Paper presented at the Twelfth Investment Treaty Forum "Investment Treaties at 50: Host State Perspectives". London (15 May), mimeo..

Schlemmer, Engela C. (2008). "Investment, investor, nationality and shareholders", in Peter Muchlinski, Federico Ortino and Christoph Schreuer (eds.), *The Oxford Handbook of International Investment Law* (Oxford: Oxford University Press), pp. 49–88.

Schreuer, Christoph, Malintoppi, Loretta, Reinisch, August and Sinclair, Anthony (2009). *The ICSID Convention: A Commentary* (Cambridge: Cambridge University Press).

Sornarajah, M. (2004). *The International Law on Foreign Investment* (Cambridge: Cambridge University Press).

United Nations Conference in Trade and Development (UNCTAD) (1999). *Scope and Definition. UNCTAD Series on Issues in International Investment Agreements* (New York and Geneva; United Nations), United Nations publication, Sales No. E.99.II.D.9, available at: http://www.unctad.org/en/docs/psiteiitd11v2.en.pdf.

_____ (2002). *World Investment Report 2002: Transnational Corporations and Export Competitiveness* (New York and Geneva; United Nations), United Nations publication, Sales No. E.02.II.D.4, available at: http://www.unctad.org/ en/docs//wir2002_en.pdf.

_____ (2003). *World Investment Report 2003. FDI Policies for Development: National and International Perspectives* (New York and Geneva; United Nations), United Nations publication, Sales No. E.03.II.D.8, available at http://www.unctad.org/en/docs/wir2003_en.pdf.

_____ (2004). *World Investment Report 2004: The Shift Towards Services* (New York and Geneva; United Nations), United Nations publication, Sales No. E.04.II.D.33, available at: http://www.unctad.org/en/docs/wir2004_en.pdf.

_____ (2005a). *World Investment Report 2005: Transnational Corporations and the Internationalization of R&D* (New York and Geneva; United Nations), United Nations publication, Sales No. E.05.II.D.10, available at: http://www.unctad.org/en/docs/wir2005_en.pdf.

_____ (2005b). *International Investment Agreements in Services. UNCTAD Series on International Investment Policies for Development* (New York and Geneva; United Nations), United Nations publication, Sales No. E.05.II.D.15, available at: http://www.unctad.org/en/docs/iteiit20052_en.pdf.

_____ (2007a). *Bilateral Investment Treaties 1995-2006: Trends in Investment Rulemaking* (New York and Geneva; United Nations), United Nations publication, Sales No. E.06.II.D.16, available at: http://www.unctad.org/en/docs/iteiia20065_en.pdf.

_____ (2007b). *Investor–State Dispute Settlement and Impact on Investment Rulemaking. UNCTAD Series on International Investment Policies for Development* (New York and Geneva; United Nations), United Nations publication, Sales No. E.07.II.D.10, available at: http://www.unctad.org/en/docs/iteiia20073_en.pdf.

_____ (2009). *The Role of International Investment Agreements in Attracting Foreign Direct Investment to Developing Countries* (New York and Geneva; United Nations), United Nations publication, Sales No. E.06.II.D.20, available at: http://www.unctad.org/en/docs/diaeia20095_en.pdf.

_____ (2010). *World Investment Report 2010. Investing in a Low-carbon Economy* (New York and Geneva: United Nations), United Nations Publication, Sales No. E.10.II.D.2, available at: http://www.unctad.org/en/docs/wir2010_en.pdf

Westcott, Thomas (2008). "CARIFORUM EPA and beyond: Recommendations for negotiations on services and trade related issues. The CARIFORUM-EU EPA and Interim Agreement between Other-ACP Regions and the EU: Investment Provisions and Commitments", Working Paper, available at: http://vi.unctad.org/files/wksp/iiawksp08/docs/wednesday/Background%20documents/westcotteucariforumepa2008.pdf.

CASES AND ARBITRAL AWARDS

ADC v. Hungary, ICSID Case No. ARB/03/16, Award, 2 October 2006.

Aguas del Tunari v. Bolivia, ICSID Case No. ARB/02/3, Decision on Jurisdiction, 21 October 2005 20 (*ICSID Review-Foreign Investment Law Journal* 450 (2005)).

AMTO v. Ukraine, Arbitration Institute of the Stockholm Chamber of Commerce, Arbitration No. 080/2005, Award, 26 March 2008. See http://www.investmenttreatynews.org/documents/p/37.aspx.

Autopista v. Venezuela, ICSID Case No. ARB/00/5, Decision on Jurisdiction, 27 September 2001, (16 *ICSID Review-Foreign Investment Law Journal* 469 (2001)).

Banro American Resources et al. v. Congo, ICSID Case ARB/98/7, Award, 1 September 2000 (excerpts) (17 *ICSID Review-Foreign Investment Law Journal* 382 (2002)).

Barcelona Traction, Light and Power Company, Limited (Belgium v. Spain), ICJ, 1970, Judgement, 24 July 1964; Judgement, 5 February 1970 (International Court of Justice Reports, 1970, pp. 3-357).

Bayindir v. Pakistan, ICSID Case No. Arb/03/29, Decision on Jurisdiction, 14 November 2005.

Biwater v. Tanzania, ICSID Case No. ARB/05/22, Award, 24 July 2008.

Ceskoslovenska Obchodni Banka, A.S. v. The Slovak Republic, Decision on Jurisdiction, 24 May 1999 (14 *ICSID Review-Foreign Investment Law Journal* 251 (1999)).

Champion Trading Company and others v. Arab Republic of Egypt, ICSID No. Arb/02/9, Decision on Jurisdiction, 21 October 2003.

CME Czech Republic v. Czech Republic, UNCITRAL, Final Award, 14 March 2003.

CMS Gas Transmission Co v. Argentina, ICSID Case No. ARB/01/8, Decision on Jurisdiction, 17 July 2003 (42 *International Legal Materials* 788 (2003)).

Company X v. State A, News from ICSID, Vol. 2 No. 2, Summer 1985.

Desert Line Projects LLC v. Yemen, ICSID Case No. ARB/05/17, Award, 6 February 2008.

EnCana v. Ecuador, UNCITRAL, Arbitration Award of the London Court of International Arbitration, 3 February 2006.

Fedax v. Venezuela, ICSID Case No. Arb/96/3, Decision on Jurisdiction, 11 July 1997 (37 *International Legal Materials* 1378 (1998)).

Fraport AG Frankfurt Airport Services Worldwide v. The Philippines, ICSID Case No. Arb/03/25, Award, 16 August 2007. See http://ita.law.uvic.ca/documents/FraportAward.pdf.

Global Trading Resource Corp. and Globex International, Inc. v. Ukraine, ICSID Case No. ARB/09/11, Award, 1 December 2010.

Hussein Nuaman Soufraki v. The United Arab Emirates, ICSID Case No. Arb/02/7 7, Award, July 2004.

Inceysa Vallisoletana, S.L. v. Republic of El Salvador, ICSID Case No. ARB/03/26, Award, 2 August 2006.

Ioannis Kardassopoulos v. Georgia, ICSID Case No. ARB/05/18, Decision on Jurisdiction, 6 July 2007.

Jan de Nul v. Egypt, ICSID Case No. ARB/04/13, Decision on Jurisdiction, 16 June 2006.

Joy Mining v. Egypt, ICSID Case No. ARB/03/11, Decision on Jurisdiction, 6 August 2004; Award on Jurisdiction, 6 August 2004 (44 *International Legal Materials* 73 (2005)). See http://ita.law.uvic.ca/documents/JoyMining_Egypt.pdf.

Lauder v. Czech Republic, UNCITRAL, Final Award, 3 September 2001.

LESI-Dipenta v. Algeria, ICSID Case No. ARB/03/8, Decision on Jurisdiction, 12 July 2006.

Loewen v. United States, ICSID Case No.ARB(AF)/98/3, Award, 26 June 2003 (42 *International Law Materials* 811 (2003)).

Maffezini v. Spain, ICSID Case No. Arb/97/7, Decision on Objections to Jurisdiction, 25 January 2000 (16 *ICSID Review-Foreign Investment Law Journal* 212 (2001)).

Malaysian Historical Salvors v. Malaysia, ICSID Case No. ARB/05/10, Award, 17 May 2007; Annulment Decision, 16 April 2009; Dissenting Opinion, 16 April 2009.

Micula v. Romania, ICSID Case No. ARB/05/20, Decision on Jurisdiction and Admissibility, 24 September 2008. See http://ita.law.uvic.ca/documents/Miculav.RomaniaJurisdiction. pdf.

Mihaly v. Sri Lanka, ICSID Case No.ARB/00/2, Award and Concurring Opinion, 15 March 2002 (41 *International Legal Materials* 867 (2002)).

Mytilineos Holdings SA v. The State Union of Serbia & Montenegro and Republic of Serbia, UNCITRAL, Partial Award, 8 September 2006.

Nagel v. Czech Republic, SCC Case 49/2002.

Nottebohm Case (Liechtenstein v. Guatemala), ICJ, Judgement, 18 November 1953; Judgement, 6 April 1955 (*International Court of Justice Reports*, 1955, pp. 4-65).

Pantechniki S.A. Contractors & Engineers v. Albania, ICSID Case No. ARB/07/21, Award, 30 July 2009.

Patrick Mitchell v. Democratic Republic of Congo, ICSID Case No.ARB/99/7, Decision on Annulment, 1 November 2006.

Petroleum Development Limited v. Sheikh of Abu Dhabi, Judgement (*International Law Reports*, 1951, Vol. 18, pp. 144-164).

Phoenix Action Ltd v. Czech Republic, ICSID Case No. ARB/06/5, Award, 15 April 2009.

Plama Consortium Limited v. Bulgaria, ICSID Case No. Arb/03/24, Decision on Jurisdiction, 8 February 2005 (44 *International Legal Materials* 721 (2005)); Award, 27 August 2008.

PSEG v. Turkey, ICSID Case No. ARB/02/5. Decision on Jurisdiction, 4 June 2004 (44 *International Legal Materials* 465 (2005)).

Romak S.A v. Uzbekistan, PCA Case No. AA280, Award, 26 November 2009. See http://ita.law.uvic.ca/documents/ROMAK-UZBEKISTANAward26November2009.pdf.

Rompetrol v. Romania, ICSID Case No. ARB/06/3, Decision on Jurisdiction, 18 April 2008.

Ruler of Qatar v. International Marine Oil Company Limited, Judgement (*International Law Reports*, 1953, Vol. 20: 534-547).

Rumeli Telekom a.s. and Telsim Mobil Telekomikasyon Hizmetleri a.s v. Republic of Kazakhstan, ICSID Case No. ARB/05/16, Award, 29 July 2008.

Saipem Spa v. Bangladesh, ICSID Case No. ARB/05/7, Decision on Jurisdiction, 21 March 2007.

Salini Costruttori SpA and Italstrade Spa v. Kingdom of Morocco, ICSID Case No. ARB/00/4, Decision on Jurisdiction, 23 July 2001 (42 *International Legal Materials* 609 (2003)).

Saluka Investments BV v. Czech Republic, UNCITRAL, Partial Award, 17 March 2006. See http://ita.law.uvic.ca/documents/Saluka-PartialawardFinal.pdf.

Sapphire International Petroleum Limited v. National Iranian Oil Company, Judgement (*International Law Reports*, 1967, Vol. 27: 117–233).

Saudi Arabia v. Arabian American Oil Company (ARAMCO), Judgement (*International Law Reports*, 1963, Vol. 27:117–233).

SOABI v. Senegal, ICSID Case ARB/82/1, Decision on Jurisdiction, 1 August 1984, (2 *ICSID Reports* 175).

Tokios Tokelés v. Ukraine, ICSID Case No. ARB/02/18, Decision on Jurisdiction, 29 April 2004 (20 *ICSID Review-Foreign Investment Law Journal* 205 (2005)); Dissenting Opinion, 29 April 2004 (20 *ICSID Review-Foreign Investment Law Journal* 245 (2005)); Award, 26 July 2007.

TSA Spectrum de Argentina S.A. v. Argentine Republic, ICSID Case No. ARB/05/5, Award, 19 December 2008.

Vacuum Salt v. Ghana, ICSID Case No. ARB/92/1, Award, 16 February 1994 (9 *ICSID Review-Foreign Investment Law Journal* 72 (1994)).

Veteran Petroleum Limited (Cyprus) v. The Russian Federation, UNCITRAL, PCA Case No. AA 228, Interim Award on Jurisdiction and Admissibility, 30 November 2009.

Victor Pey Casado and President Allende Foundation v. Republic of Chile, ICSID Case No. ARB/98/2, Award, 8 May 2008.

Waguih Elie George Siag and Clorinda Vecchi v. The Arab Republic of Egypt, ICSID Case No. Arb/05/15, Decision on Jurisdiction, 11 April 2007. See http://ita.law.uvic.ca/documents/Siagv.Egypt.pdf.

Waste Management v. Mexico, ICSID Case No. ARB(AF)/00/3, Award, 30 April 2004 (43 International Legal Materials 967 (2004)).

SELECTED UNCTAD PUBLICATIONS ON INTERNATIONAL INVESTMENT AGREEMENTS, TRANSNATIONAL CORPORATIONS AND FOREIGN DIRECT INVESTMENT

(For more information, please visit www.unctad.org/en/pub)

World Investment Reports
(For more information visit www.unctad.org/wir)

World Investment Report 2010. Investing in a Low-Carbon Economy. Sales No. E.10.II.D.1. $80. http://www.unctad.org/en/docs//wir2010_en.pdf.

World Investment Report 2009. Transnational Corporations, Agricultural Production and Development. Sales No. E.09.II.D.15. $80. http://www.unctad.org/en/docs/wir2009_en.pdf.

World Investment Report 2008. Transnational Corporations and the Infrastructure Challenge. Sales No. E.08.II.D.23. $80. http://www.unctad.org/en/docs//wir2008_en.pdf.

World Investment Report 2007. Transnational Corporations, Extractive Industries and Development. Sales No. E.07.II.D.9. $75. http://www.unctad.org/en/docs//wir2007_en.pdf.

World Investment Report 2006. FDI from Developing and Transition Economies: Implications for Development. Sales No. E.06.II.D.11. $75. http://www.unctad.org/ en/docs//wir2006_en.pdf.

World Investment Report 2005. Transnational Corporations and the Internationalization of R&D. Sales No. E.05.II.D.10. $75. http://www.unctad.org/ en/docs//wir2005_en.pdf.

World Investment Report 2004. The Shift Towards Services. Sales No. E.04.II.D.36. $75. http://www.unctad.org/en/docs//wir2004_en.pdf.

World Investment Report 2003. FDI Policies for Development: National and International Perspectives. Sales No. E.03.II.D.8. $49. http://www.unctad.org/en/docs//wir2003_en.pdf.

World Investment Report 2002: Transnational Corporations and Export Competitiveness. 352 p. Sales No. E.02.II.D.4. $49. http://www.unctad.org/en/docs//wir2002_en.pdf.

World Investment Report 2001: Promoting Linkages. 356 p. Sales No. E.01.II.D.12 $49. http://www.unctad.org/wir/contents/wir01content.en.htm.

World Investment Report 2000: Cross-border Mergers and Acquisitions and Development. 368 p. Sales No. E.99.II.D.20. $49. http://www.unctad.org/wir/contents/wir00content.en.htm.

Ten Years of World Investment Reports: The Challenges Ahead. Proceedings *of an UNCTAD special event on future challenges in the area of FDI.* UNCTAD/ITE/Misc.45. http://www.unctad.org/wir.

International Investment Policies for Development
(For more information visit http://www.unctad.org/iia)

Investor-State Disputes: Prevention and Alternatives to Arbitration, 129 p. Sales No. E.10.II.D.11. $20.

The Role of International Investment Agreements in Attracting Foreign Direct Investment to Developing Countries. 161 p. Sales No. E.09.II.D.20. $22.

The Protection of National Security in IIAs. 170 p. Sales No. E.09.II.D.12. $15.

Identifying Core Elements in Investment Agreements in the APEC Regions. 134 p. Sales No. E.08.II.D.27. $15.

International Investment Rule-Making: Stocktaking, Challenges and the Way Forward. 124 p. Sales No. E.08.II.D.1. $15.

Investment Promotion Provisions in International Investment Agreements. 103 p. Sales No. E.08.II.D.5. $15.

Investor-State Dispute Settlement and Impact on Investment Rulemaking. 110 p. Sales No. E.07.II.D.10. $30.

Bilateral Investment Treaties 1995—2006: Trends in Investment Rulemaking. 172 p. Sales No. E.06.II.D.16. $30.

Investment Provisions in Economic Integration Agreements. 174 p. UNCTAD/ITE/IIT/2005/10.

Preserving Flexibility in IIAs: The Use of Reservations. 104 p. Sales No. E.06.II.D.14. $15.

International Investment Arrangements: Trends and Emerging Issues. 110 p. Sales No. E.06.II.D.03. $15.

Investor-State Disputes Arising from Investment Treaties: A Review. 106 p. Sales No. E.06.II.D.1 $15

South-South Cooperation in Investment Arrangements. 108 p. Sales No. E.05.II.D.26 $15.

International Investment Agreements in Services. 119 p. Sales No. E.05.II.D.15. $15.

The REIO Exception in MFN Treatment Clauses. 92 p. Sales No. E.05.II.D.1. $15.

Issues in International Investment Agreements
(For more information visit http://www.unctad.org/iia)

Most-Favoured-Nation Treatment: A Sequel. 141 p. Sales No. E.10.II.D.19. $25

International Investment Agreements: Key Issues, Volumes I, II and *III.* Sales no.: E.05.II.D.6. $65.

State Contracts. 84 p. Sales No. E.05.II.D.5. $15.

Competition. 112 p. Sales No. E.04.II.D.44. $ 15.

Key Terms and Concepts in IIAs: a Glossary. 232 p. Sales No. E.04.II.D.31. $15.

Incentives. 108 p. Sales No. E.04.II.D.6. $15.

Transparency. 118 p. Sales No. E.04.II.D.7. $15.

Dispute Settlement: State-State. 101 p. Sales No. E.03.II.D.6. $15.

Dispute Settlement: Investor-State. 125 p. Sales No. E.03.II.D.5. $15.

Transfer of Technology. 138 p. Sales No. E.01.II.D.33. $18.

Illicit Payments. 108 p. Sales No. E.01.II.D.20. $13.

Home Country Measures. 96 p. Sales No.E.01.II.D.19. $12.

Host Country Operational Measures. 109 p. Sales No E.01.II.D.18. $15.

Social Responsibility. 91 p. Sales No. E.01.II.D.4. $15.

Environment. 105 p. Sales No. E.01.II.D.3. $15.

Transfer of Funds. 68 p. Sales No. E.00.II.D.27. $12.

Flexibility for Development. 185 p. Sales No. E.00.II.D.6. $15.

Employment. 69 p. Sales No. E.00.II.D.15. $12.

Taxation. 111 p. Sales No. E.00.II.D.5. $12.

Taking of Property. 83 p. Sales No. E.00.II.D.4. $12.

National Treatment.. 94 p. Sales No. E.99.II.D.16. $12.

Admission and Establishment.. 69 p. Sales No. E.99.II.D.10. $12.

Trends in International Investment Agreements: An Overview. 133 p. Sales No. E.99.II.D.23. $12.

Lessons from the MAI. 52 p. Sales No. E.99.II.D.26. $10.

Fair and Equitable Treatment.. 85 p. Sales No. E.99.II.D.15. $12.

Transfer Pricing.. 71 p. Sales No. E.99.II.D.8. $12.

Scope and Definition. 93 p. Sales No. E.99.II.D.9. $12.

Most-Favoured Nation Treatment.. 57 p. Sales No. E.99.II.D.11. $12.

Investment-Related Trade Measures. 57 p. Sales No. E.99.II.D.12. $12.

Foreign Direct Investment and Development.. 74 p. Sales No. E.98.II.D.15. $12.

Investment Policy Monitors

Investment Policy Monitor. A Periodic Report by the UNCTAD Secretariat. No. 3, 7 October 2010.
http://www.unctad.org/en/docs/webdiaeia20105_en.pdf

Investment Policy Monitor. A Periodic Report by the UNCTAD Secretariat. No. 2, 20 April 2010.
http://www.unctad.org/en/docs/webdiaeia20102_en.pdf

Investment Policy Monitor. A Periodic Report by the UNCTAD Secretariat. No. 1, 4 December 2009.
http://www.unctad.org/en/docs/webdiaeia200911_en.pdf

IIA Monitors and Issues Notes

IIA Issues Note No. 1 (2010): Latest Developments in Investor–State Dispute Settlement.
http://www.unctad.org/en/docs/webdiaeia20103_en.pdf

IIA Monitor No. 3 (2009): Recent developments in international investment agreements (2008–June 2009).
http://www.unctad.org/en/docs/webdiaeia20098_en.pdf

IIA Monitor No. 2 (2009): Selected Recent Developments in IIA Arbitration and Human Rights.
http://www.unctad.org/en/docs/webdiaeia20097_en.pdf

IIA Monitor No. 1 (2009): Latest Developments in Investor-State Dispute Settlement.
http://www.unctad.org/en/docs/webdiaeia20096_en.pdf

IIA Monitor No. 2 (2008): Recent developments in international investment agreements (2007–June 2008).
http://www.unctad.org/en/docs/webdiaeia20081_en.pdf

IIA Monitor No. 1 (2008): Latest Developments in Investor– State Dispute Settlement.
http://www.unctad.org/en/docs/iteiia20083_en.pdf

IIA Monitor No. 3 (2007): Recent developments in international investment agreements (2006 – June 2007).
http://www.unctad.org/en/docs/webiteiia20076_en.pdf

IIA Monitor No. 2 (2007): Development implications of international investment agreements.
http://www.unctad.org/en/docs/webiteiia20072_en.pdf

IIA Monitor No. 1 (2007): Intellectual Property Provisions in International Investment Arrangements.
http://www.unctad.org/en/docs/webiteiia20071_en.pdf

IIA Monitor No. 4 (2006): Latest Developments in Investor-State Dispute Settlement.
http://www.unctad.org/sections/dite_pcbb/docs/webiteiia200611_en.pdf

IIA Monitor No. 3 (2006): The Entry into Force of Bilateral Investment Treaties (BITs).
http://www.unctad.org/en/docs/webiteiia20069_en.pdf

IIA Monitor No. 2 (2006): Developments in international investment agreements in 2005.
http://www.unctad.org/en/docs/webiteiia20067_en.pdf

IIA Monitor No. 1 (2006): Systemic Issues in International Investment Agreements (IIAs).
http://www.unctad.org/en/docs/webiteiia20062_en.pdf

IIA Monitor No. 4 (2005): Latest Developments in Investor-State Dispute Settlement.
http://www.unctad.org/en/docs/webiteiit20052_en.pdf

IIA Monitor No. 2 (2005): Recent Developments in International Investment Agreements.
http://www.unctad.org/en/docs/webiteiit20051_en.pdf

IIA Monitor No. 1 (2005): South-South Investment Agreements Proliferating.
http://www.unctad.org/en/docs/webiteiit20061_en.pdf

United Nations publications may be obtained from bookstores and distributors throughout the world. Please consult your bookstore or write:

For Africa, Asia and Europe to:

Sales Section
United Nations Office at Geneva
Palais des Nations
CH-1211 Geneva 10
Switzerland
Tel: (41-22) 917-1234
Fax: (41-22) 917-0123
E-mail: unpubli@unog.ch

For Asia and the Pacific, the Caribbean, Latin America and North America to:

Sales Section
Room DC2-0853
United Nations Secretariat
New York, NY 10017
United States
Tel: (1-212) 963-8302 or (800) 253-9646
Fax: (1-212) 963-3489
E-mail: publications@un.org

All prices are quoted in United States dollars.

For further information on the work of the Division on Investment and Enterprise, UNCTAD, please address inquiries to:

United Nations Conference on Trade and Development
Division on Investment and Enterprise
Palais des Nations, Room E-10054
CH-1211 Geneva 10, Switzerland
Telephone: (41-22) 917-5651
Telefax: (41-22) 917-0498
http://www.unctad.org

QUESTIONNAIRE

Scope and Definition: A Sequel
Sales No. E.10.II.D.

In order to improve the quality and relevance of the work of the UNCTAD Division on Investment, Technology and Enterprise Development, it would be useful to receive the views of readers on this publication. It would therefore be greatly appreciated if you could complete the following questionnaire and return it to:

Readership Survey
UNCTAD Division on Investment and Enterprise
United Nations Office at Geneva
Palais des Nations, Room E-9123
CH-1211 Geneva 10, Switzerland
Fax: 41-22-917-0194

1. Name and address of respondent (optional):

_____

_____

2. Which of the following best describes your area of work?

Government ☐   Public enterprise ☐

Private enterprise ☐   Academic or research institution ☐

International organization ☐   Media ☐

Not-for-profit organization ☐   Other (specify) _____

3. In which country do you work? _____

4. What is your assessment of the contents of this publication?

Excellent ☐ Adequate ☐
Good ☐ Poor ☐

5. How useful is this publication to your work?

Very useful ☐ Somewhat useful ☐
Irrelevant ☐

6. Please indicate the three things you liked best about this publication:

_____

_____

_____

7. Please indicate the three things you liked least about this publication:

_____

_____

_____

8. If you have read other publications of the UNCTAD Division on Investment, Enterprise Development and Technology, what is your overall assessment of them?

Consistently good ☐ Usually good, but with
some exceptions ☐
Generally mediocre ☐ Poor ☐

9. On average, how useful are those publications to you in your work?

Very useful   ☐   Somewhat useful   ☐

Irrelevant   ☐

10. Are you a regular recipient of *Transnational Corporations* (formerly *The CTC Reporter*), UNCTAD-DITE's tri-annual refereed journal?

Yes ☐   No ☐

If not, please check here if you would like to receive a sample copy sent to the name and address you have given above: ☐